Teacher Edition

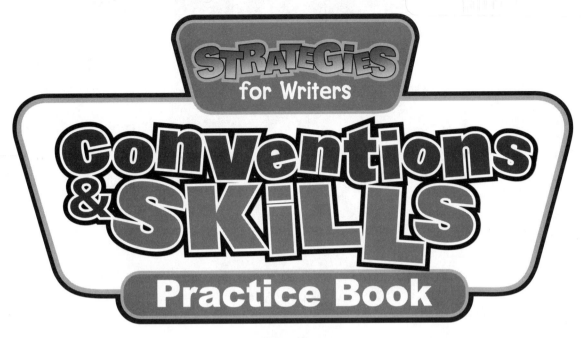

STRATEGIES for Writers

Conventions & SKILLS
Practice Book

Level F

Authors

Leslie W. Crawford, Ed.D.
Georgia College & State University

Rebecca Bowers Sipe, Ed.D.
Eastern Michigan University

Editorial Development by Cottage Communications

Cover Design by Tommaso Design Group

Production by Marilyn Rodgers Bahney Paselsky

Copyright © Zaner-Bloser, Inc.

Zaner-Bloser, Inc., P.O. Box 16764, Columbus, Ohio 43216-6764 (1-800-421-3018)

ISBN 0-7367-1260-7

Printed in the United States of America

02   03   04   05   06   MZ   5   4   3   2   1

Table of Contents

Unit 1
Sentence Structure

Unit 2
Parts of Speech

Unit 3

Usage

Unit 4

Grammar

Unit 5
Mechanics

Complete Subjects and Complete Predicates

Learn

Delegates I met for an important vote.
    a.   **b.**

Which part of this sentence, **a.** or **b.**, tells whom or what the sentence is about? _____ a. _____

Which part of this sentence tells what happened? _____ b. _____

> Every sentence has a subject and a predicate. The **complete subject** is made up of a noun or a pronoun and words that tell about it. The subject tells whom or what the sentence is about. The **complete predicate** is made up of a verb and words that tell what the subject is, has, or does.

Practice

Underline the complete subject in each sentence. Circle each complete predicate.

1. The only state smaller than Delaware is Rhode Island.

2. Delaware measures just 96 miles from north to south.

3. Its greatest east-to-west distance is even shorter.

4. Delaware's delegates approved the United States Constitution before any other delegates.

5. John Dickinson and George Read of Delaware helped with the writing of the Constitution.

6. The small state of Delaware claims the title "First State." It claims other firsts.

7. The first Christmas seals in the United States went on sale in Wilmington, Delaware.

8. The first beauty contest in the United States took place at Rehoboth Beach in Delaware.

Add a subject or a predicate to each phrase to make a sentence. Underline the complete subject in each sentence. **Answers will vary.**

9. Tiny Delaware _____

_____

10. were sold in Delaware. _____

_____

11. Distances in Delaware _____

_____

12. George Read _____

_____

13. also helped in the writing. _____

_____

14. is less than 40 miles wide. _____

_____

15. Rehoboth Beach _____

_____

16. Rhode Island _____

_____

17. The United States Constitution _____

_____

18. Wilmington, Delaware _____

_____

Simple Subjects, Simple Predicates; Understood *You*

Learn

A well-known explorer (visited) the Hawaiian Islands in 1778.

Underline the most important word in the subject. Circle the verb.

Guess how many people live in Hawaii.

Can you find a subject at the beginning of this sentence? _____no_____
Circle the word that fits as the subject of the sentence.   people   (you)   Hawaii

> The **simple subject** is the most important word or words in the complete subject. It is a noun or pronoun and tells whom or what the sentence is about. The subject of a request or command is usually not named. **You** (the person being spoken to) is the **understood subject**. The **simple predicate** is the most important word or words in the complete predicate. It is a verb. The simple predicate tells what the subject did or what was done to the subject. It may also be a form of the verb *be*.

Practice

Write the simple subject (including **you**) in each sentence. Circle each simple predicate.

1. The state of Hawaii (is) the only island state.   ___state___

2. Polynesians (sailed) to Hawaii in giant canoes.   ___Polynesians___

3. Captain James Cook (landed) in Hawaii in 1778.   ___Captain James Cook___

4. King Kamehameha I (unified) Hawaii.   ___King Kamehameha I___

5. (Think) of what Hawaii is like now.   ___you___

6. Sugar cane (grows) between Maui's volcanoes.   ___Sugar cane___

7. (Guess) why Lanai is "the Pineapple Island."   ___you___

8. The Hawaiian alphabet (has) only 12 letters.   ___alphabet___

9. Hawaii (joined) the union in 1959.   ___Hawaii___

Write a sentence to answer each question below. Circle the simple subject and underline the simple predicate. Use the understood **you** in one sentence. **Answers will vary.**

10. When did Hawaii become a state? _____

_____

11. How did the Polynesians get to Hawaii? _____

_____

12. Did Hawaii ever have kings? _____

_____

13. Who visited the islands in 1778? _____

_____

14. Who was the first king of Hawaii? _____

_____

15. How does Hawaii differ from other states? _____

_____

16. Is there anything unusual about the Hawaiian alphabet? _____

_____

17. When did Hawaii become one of the United States? _____

_____

18. What advice would you give someone thinking of visiting Hawaii? _____

_____

19. What could you do when visiting Hawaii? _____

_____

20. The battleship *Arizona* in Pearl Harbor is a memorial to what? _____

_____

Compound Subjects and Compound Predicates

Learn

Cowboys and cattle symbolize Texas to many. ____S____

Texans also program computers and track spacecraft. ____P____

Write **S** next to the sentence with two or more simple subjects.
Write **P** next to the sentence with two or more simple predicates.

> A **compound subject** is two or more subjects joined by a conjunction
> (*and, or*). A **compound predicate** contains two or more verbs joined by
> a conjunction.

Practice

Each sentence below has either a compound subject or a compound predicate. Underline
the words that make up each compound subject. Circle the verbs in each compound predicate.

1. Alaska and Texas are our two largest states.

2. Many Texans boasted and bragged that their state was the largest before Alaska
   became a state in 1959.

3. Texas is now the second largest state and has many interesting features.

4. People fish, swim, and sail along the beautiful Gulf Coast.

5. Farmers raise cattle and cultivate fruit on the Coastal Plains.

6. Oaks and pines are plentiful in the Gulf Coastal Plains.

7. Once, Comanches and Tonkawas inhabited Texas.

8. The Spanish explored and built missions in Texas.

9. Both the French and the Spanish tried to get a foothold in the land that became Texas.

10. The United States and France completed the Louisiana Purchase in 1803.

Apply

Combine each set of sentences to make a new sentence that has either a compound subject or a compound predicate. **Answers may vary. Possible responses appear below.**

11. Comanches clashed with the settlers of the new Republic of Texas. Mexicans also clashed with Texans.

    Comanches and Mexicans clashed with the settlers of the new Republic of Texas.

12. Texans elected a president. They also voted to join the United States.

    Texans elected a president and voted to join the United States.

13. The Senate approved statehood for Texas in 1845. The House of Representatives also approved statehood.

    The Senate and the House of Representatives approved statehood for Texas in 1845.

14. The new state of Texas kept its public lands. It paid its own debts.

    The new state of Texas kept its public lands and paid its own debts.

15. Many Texans moved from the country to the cities after World War II. They found jobs in factories and other growing industries.

    Many Texans moved from the country to the cities after World War II and found jobs in factories

    and other growing industries.

16. NASA provides many jobs in the Houston area. The area also is the home of the busy Port of Houston.

    NASA and the Port of Houston provide many jobs in the Houston area.

Copyright © Zaner-Bloser, Inc.

Name _____

Direct and Indirect Objects

Learn

The Native Americans taught the Pilgrims many (things).

Circle the noun that tells what Native Americans taught. Underline the noun that tells to whom they taught it.

> The **direct object** is the noun or pronoun that receives the action of the verb. Only action verbs can take a direct object. A **compound direct object** occurs when more than one noun or pronoun receives the action of the verb. The **indirect object** is a thing or person to whom something is given, told, or taught. The indirect object is a noun or pronoun, and it comes before the direct object. To test whether a word is an indirect object, move it after the direct object and put the word *to* in front of it.

Practice

Underline each direct object. Circle each indirect object. Not every sentence has an indirect object.

1. The Pilgrims have given (Massachusetts) a place in American history.

2. However, other Europeans first saw Massachusetts.

3. Bartholomew Gosnold gave (Cape Cod) its name in 1602.

4. A book by John Smith gave the (Pilgrims) guidance.

5. They sailed their ships to Plymouth in 1620.

6. Winter caused the (Pilgrims) great hardship.

7. The Puritans founded a colony on Massachusetts Bay.

8. The location of the Puritan settlement provided (Massachusetts) the nickname "The Bay State."

9. Early historic figures have brought some (cities) special recognition.

10. Paul Revere has given (Lexington) and (Concord) special fame.

Apply

Complete these sentences by adding a direct object or a direct object and an indirect object.

11. Native Americans gave _____

_____

12. In 1620, the Pilgrims saw _____

_____

13. The Pilgrims needed _____

_____

14. The leader of the group sent _____

_____

15. The settlers named _____

_____

16. The first winter claimed _____

_____

17. Paul Revere warned _____

_____

18. The Puritans told _____

_____

19. Native Americans taught _____

_____

20. Massachusetts provided _____

_____

Predicate Nouns and Predicate Adjectives

Learn

The thirty-eighth state admitted to the United States was **Colorado**.
Most people say that Colorado is quite **beautiful**.

Which boldfaced word tells who or what the subject is? _____ Colorado _____

Which boldfaced word describes the subject? _____ beautiful _____

> A **predicate noun** follows a linking verb and renames the subject.
> A **predicate adjective** follows a linking verb and describes the subject.

Practice

Write **PN** if the boldfaced word is a predicate noun. Write **PA** if the boldfaced word is a predicate adjective.

1. The first Colorado mountain valley dwellers were the **Utes**. ___PN___

2. Ute houses were **cone shaped**. ___PA___

3. The first European explorers were the **Spanish**. ___PN___

4. They were **disappointed** when they did not find gold. ___PA___

5. The next explorers were the **French**. ___PN___

6. Many were **trappers** and **hunters**. ___PN___

7. The event that brought many settlers to Colorado was the **Gold Rush**. ___PN___

8. One of four U.S. mints for producing coins is the **Denver Mint**. ___PN___

9. A mint in Denver seems **appropriate**. ___PA___

10. The mining of gold and silver in Colorado was **important** in the 1850s. ___PA___

Apply

Write a predicate adjective or a predicate noun to complete each sentence. You may use words from the Word Bank.

Word Bank

"Centennial State"	important	"colored red"	columbine	1876
reason	animal	word	team	famous
largest	popular	red	younger	

11. The state name, *Colorado*, is a Spanish _____word_____ .

12. The meaning of the word is _____"colored red"_____ .

13. The color of the Colorado River is the _____reason_____ for its name.

14. The Colorado River appears _____red_____ as it flows through canyons.

15. The state's nickname is the _____"Centennial State"_____ .

16. The year of Colorado statehood is _____1876_____ .

17. Colorado is _____younger_____ than the nation by 100 years.

18. Locations in the Rocky Mountains of Colorado have become _____popular_____ for vacations.

19. Agriculture, manufacturing, mining, and tourism are _____important_____ in Colorado's economy.

20. A silver nugget found in 1894 in Aspen, Colorado, was the _____largest_____ ever found in North America.

21. The Rocky Mountain bighorn sheep is the official _____animal_____ of Colorado.

22. The Colorado state flower is the _____columbine_____ .

23. Buffalo Bill is one _____famous_____ person who is buried in Colorado.

24. The Colorado Rapids is a professional soccer _____team_____ .

Prepositional Phrases

Learn

Hopeful gold miners rushed to California in 1849.

Where did the gold miners rush? _____ to California _____

When did they rush there? _____ in 1849 _____

> A **prepositional phrase** can tell *how, what kind, when, how much,* or *where*. A prepositional phrase begins with a **preposition**, such as *in, over, of, to,* or *by*. It ends with a noun or pronoun that is the **object of the preposition**. The words between the preposition and its object are part of the prepositional phrase. A prepositional phrase can appear at the beginning, middle, or end of a sentence.

Practice

Put parentheses around each prepositional phrase. Draw a line under the preposition that begins each phrase. There may be more than one prepositional phrase in each sentence.

1. California was named (<u>by</u> Spanish explorers) (<u>in</u> the 1500s.)

2. The place reminded the explorers (<u>of</u> a Spanish story) (<u>about</u> a treasure island.)

3. California's nickname, "The Golden State," comes (<u>from</u> the history) (<u>of</u> gold mining.)

4. Gold was discovered (<u>in</u> 1848) (<u>by</u> John Sutter.)

5. The news (<u>of</u> his discovery) spread very fast.

6. Gold mining hopefuls, the Forty-Niners, rushed (<u>to</u> California) (<u>in</u> 1849.)

7. They came (<u>from</u> all parts) (<u>of</u> the world.)

8. San Francisco grew (<u>from</u> a small town) (<u>to</u> a city) (<u>within</u> a year.)

9. Not all (<u>of</u> the miners) were successful.

10. There were other opportunities, though, (<u>in</u> the rich land) (<u>of</u> the valley.)

Apply

Add a preposition to each prepositional phrase and complete each sentence. You may choose prepositions from the Word Bank. You may use words more than once.

Word Bank

in	of	through	across	for	within
to	from	between	inside	on	outside
about	over	around	at	since	by

11. California's first constitution was adopted _____in_____ 1849.

12. The state governor is elected _____for_____ a four-year term.

13. The number _____of_____ terms a governor can serve is not limited.

14. There are 58 counties _____in/inside_____ California.

15. California became the thirty-first state _____on_____ September 9, 1850.

16. San Francisco was the state capital _____between_____ 1850 and 1854.

17. Sacramento has been the capital _____since_____ 1854.

18. California's reputation has gone _____from_____ being a gold site _____to_____ being a technology site.

19. Manufacturing _____of_____ computer chips and production _____of_____ films attract more people to California all the time.

20. Many people have moved _____to_____ California _____over_____ the years seeking fortune, fame, and other opportunities.

Active and Passive Voice

Learn

a. <u>New York</u> **has earned** a reputation as a major trade and manufacturing state.

b. <u>New York</u> **is known** by many people as "The Empire State."

Look at the underlined subject and the boldfaced verb in each sentence.

In which sentence, **a.** or **b.**, does the subject do something? _____a._____

In which sentence does the subject have something done to it? _____b._____

> If the subject performs an action, the verb is said to be in **active voice**. If the subject is acted upon by something else, the verb is said to be in **passive voice**. Many sentences in passive voice have a phrase beginning with the word *by*.

Practice

Underline the verb in each sentence. Write **AV** if the verb is in active voice. Write **PV** if the verb is in passive voice.

1. New York's state nickname was <u>given</u> by George Washington. _____PV_____

2. In 1783, Washington <u>called</u> New York the "possible seat of a new empire." _____AV_____

3. New York was <u>explored</u> by Henry Hudson in the early seventeenth century. _____PV_____

4. Hudson <u>sailed</u> for the Netherlands. _____AV_____

5. The area was <u>named</u> New Netherland by the government of the Netherlands. _____PV_____

6. New York City was <u>called</u> New Amsterdam by the Dutch. _____PV_____

7. Much Dutch influence <u>is</u> still <u>found</u> in New York. _____PV_____

8. The state of New York is <u>counted</u> among the thirteen original colonies. _____PV_____

9. New York's first constitution was <u>adopted</u> in 1777. _____PV_____

10. New York <u>entered</u> the union as the eleventh state in 1788. _____AV_____

Apply

Rewrite each sentence so that the verb is in active voice. You might need to rearrange words in the sentence. You might also need to add or take out words.

11. New York was explored by Giovanni da Verrazano in about 1524. _____

Giovanni da Verrazano explored New York in about 1524.

12. He was sent to North America by King Francis I of France. _____

King Francis I of France sent him to North America.

13. In 1609, northern New York was entered by the French explorer Samuel de Champlain.

The French explorer Samuel de Champlain entered northern New York in 1609.

14. A settlement called New Amsterdam was built on Manhattan by Dutch colonists in 1625.

In 1625, Dutch colonists built a settlement called New Amsterdam on Manhattan.

15. Manhattan was bought from the native people by the Dutch for 60 Dutch guilders, which equaled about 24 dollars.

The Dutch bought Manhattan from the native people for 60 Dutch guilders, which equaled about 24 dollars.

16. In 1664, the area was taken over by the English. _____

The English took over the area in 1664.

17. The settlement was surrendered to the English by the Dutch governor, Peter Stuyvesant.

The Dutch governor, Peter Stuyvesant, surrendered the settlement to the English.

18. The territory was renamed New York by the English. _____

The English renamed the territory New York.

Appositives

Learn

Montana, the fourth largest state in the nation, once belonged to France.
        a.   **b.**

Which part of the sentence, **a.** or **b.**, tells what Montana is? ____a.____
Circle the punctuation marks that separate that part from the rest of the sentence.

> An **appositive** is a phrase that identifies, or means the same thing as, a noun. Appositives follow the nouns they identify and are usually separated from the rest of the sentence by commas.

Practice

Circle the appositive in each sentence. Underline the noun the appositive identifies.

1. Montana's nickname, "The Treasure State," comes from its many minerals in the mountains of the western part of the state.

2. Another name for Montana, "Big Sky Country," comes from the view of open plains in the eastern part of the state.

3. Most of Montana was part of a large area, the Louisiana Territory, bought by the United States in 1803. Lewis and Clark explored the territory.

4. Helena, the state capital since 1875, is the third location for the state capital.

5. The main street in the capital has an unusual name, Last Chance Gulch.

6. The older Last Chance Gulch, a gold camp, used to stand where Helena is now.

7. A surprising discovery, a deposit of gold, brought both miners and outlaws to Montana in 1862.

8. Chief Joseph, a famous Native American, led his tribe through Montana.

9. A famous battlefield, a site near the Little Bighorn River, is in southeastern Montana.

10. Montana vigorously protects its forests, one of its great natural resources.

Strategies for Writers—Conventions & Skills Practice   Unit I

Write six complete sentences using the sentence parts provided for each item. Include an appositive in each sentence. Add any words you wish to make a complete sentence.

11. another feature   snow-capped mountains   gave the nickname "Land of Shining Mountains"

12. Jeannette Rankin   first woman in Congress   elected in 1916

13. explorers of the Louisiana Territory   Meriwether Lewis and William Clark   traveled through Montana in the early 1800s

14. November 8, 1889   birthday of statehood   was an important date in Montana's history

15. another important year   1973   a new state constitution went into effect

16. Grasshopper Creek   site of gold strike in 1862   brought many gold miners to the state

Answers will vary. Possible responses appear below.

11. Another feature, snow-capped mountains, gave Montana the nickname "Land of Shining Mountains."

12. The first woman in Congress, Jeannette Rankin, was elected in 1916.

13. Meriwether Lewis and William Clark, explorers of the Louisiana Territory, traveled through Montana in the early 1800s.

14. The birthday of statehood, November 8, 1889, was an important date in Montana's history.

15. A new state constitution went into effect in another important year, 1973.

16. Grasshopper Creek, the site of a gold strike in 1862, brought many gold miners to the state.

Compound and Complex Sentences

Learn

When Florida became a state, there were only 26 other states in the union. ____CX____

Spain ceded Florida to England in 1763, but Spain took control of Florida again in 1783. ____CD____

Write **CD** after the sentence that joins two sentences with a comma and a conjunction.
Write **CX** after the sentence that joins a sentence and a group of words beginning with *when*.

> An **independent clause** is a sentence that makes sense by itself. A **compound sentence** is made of two closely related independent clauses. The two clauses can be joined by a comma and a conjunction (*and, but, or*) or by a semicolon (;). A **dependent clause** has a subject and a verb, but it does not make complete sense by itself. It needs an independent clause. A dependent clause begins with a subordinating conjunction, such as *although, because, if, as,* or *when*. A **complex sentence** is made up of a dependent clause and an independent clause.

Practice

Write **CD** after each compound sentence and underline the comma and the conjunction or the semicolon. Write **CX** after each complex sentence and underline the subordinating conjunction.

1. An important date in Florida history is 1513, when Juan Ponce de León arrived. ____CX____

2. When Juan Ponce de León reached the coast of Florida, he claimed it for Spain. ____CX____

3. Florida was under the control of Spain for the next 250 years; it came under the control of England in 1763. ____CD____

4. Great Britain had control of Florida in 1763, but it gave the land back to Spain in 1783. ____CD____

5. Florida became a part of the U.S. in 1821, and it was established as a territory in 1822. ____CD____

6. Tallahassee became the capital of Florida in 1824, and it is still the capital today. ____CD____

7. Florida had been part of the U.S. for 24 years when it became a state in 1845. ____CX____

Apply

Combine each pair of simple sentences to make a compound or a complex sentence. Use a subordinating conjunction to make a complex sentence. Use a comma and a conjunction or a semicolon to make a compound sentence. **Answers will vary. Possible responses appear below.**

8. The National Aeronautics and Space Administration (NASA) looked for a site for launching satellites.
   It chose Cape Canaveral in Florida.

   The National Aeronautics and Space Administration (NASA) looked for a site for launching satellites,

   and it chose Cape Canaveral in Florida.

9. This site was called Cape Kennedy from 1963 to 1973.
   Later its name was changed back to Cape Canaveral.

   This site was called Cape Kennedy from 1963 to 1973; later its name was changed back to Cape Canaveral.

10. *Explorer I* was the first U.S. satellite to orbit the earth.
    The Soviet Union had launched a satellite a year earlier.

    Explorer I was the first U.S. satellite to orbit the earth, but the Soviet Union had launched a satellite a year earlier.

11. About five tribes of Native Americans lived in Florida.
    European explorers arrived in the sixteenth century.

    When European explorers arrived in the sixteenth century, about five tribes of Native Americans lived in Florida.

12. The first Spanish explorers heard about a fountain of youth.
    They went to Florida.

    After the first Spanish explorers heard about a fountain of youth, they went to Florida.

13. They were disappointed.
    There was no such thing.

    They were disappointed when there was no such thing.

Avoid Fragments, Run-ons, Comma Splices

Learn

  F   New Mexico the Land of Enchantment.

 CS New Mexico has great beauty, it also has a rich history.

  S   New Mexico is a state in the southwestern part of the country.

Write **S** by the complete sentence.
Write **F** by the phrase that does not give a complete thought.
Write **CS** by the sentence that needs a conjunction.

> A **fragment** does not tell a complete thought. A **run-on sentence** is two sentences that are run together without a comma and a conjunction. A **comma splice** is two sentences that are joined only by a comma but are missing a conjunction. To fix each type of incorrect sentence, add what is missing or make two separate sentences.

Practice

Write **F** after each fragment. Write **RO** after each run-on sentence. Write **CS** after each comma splice. Write **S** after each correct sentence. (**1.–12.**)

New Mexico is a land of interest to many different groups. ____**S**____ Tourists love its beauty,

historians enjoy its cultures and ancient ruins. ____**CS**____ Scientists see New Mexico as a source of

mineral resources. ____**S**____ A place to consider the old and the new. ____**F**____

Santa Fe is the capital of the state, it is the oldest seat of government in the nation. ____**CS**____

Began as a Spanish capital in 1609. ____**F**____ Spain ruled this land for many years later it

belonged to Mexico. ____**RO**____ Became part of the United States in 1848. ____**F**____ It joined the

union as the forty-seventh state in 1912. ____**S**____

Native Americans have a much longer heritage in New Mexico than do Europeans. ____**S**____

Probably have lived there for 20,000 years. ____**F**____ The ancestors of many tribes of the area are

called the Anasazi they have left some fascinating signs of their civilization. ____**RO**____

Rewrite the fragments, run-ons, and comma splices you found in the last exercise. Correct the errors.

13. Tourists love its beauty, and historians enjoy its cultures and ancient ruins.

_____

_____

14. It is a place in which to consider the old and the new.

_____

_____

15. Santa Fe is the capital of the state; it is the oldest seat of government in the nation.

_____

_____

16. Santa Fe began as a Spanish capital in 1609.

_____

_____

17. Spain ruled this land for many years. Later it belonged to Mexico.

_____

_____

18. Then New Mexico became part of the United States in 1848.

_____

_____

19. They probably have lived there for 20,000 years.

_____

_____

20. The ancestors of many tribes of the area are called the Anasazi. They have left some fascinating

signs of their civilization.

_____

Kinds of Nouns

Learn

You probably have heard of <u>Edison's</u> many <u>inventions</u> and his **laboratory** in **New Jersey**.

Which boldfaced words name a particular place or thing? _____ New Jersey _____

Which underlined word shows ownership? _____ Edison's _____

> A **common noun** names any person, place, thing, or idea. A **proper noun** names a particular person, place, thing, or idea. Proper nouns must be capitalized. A **singular noun** names one person, place, idea, or thing. A **plural noun** names more than one. Most nouns add -s or -es to form the plural. Some nouns change spelling in the plural form (*goose/geese*). Some nouns have the same singular and plural form (*deer*). A **possessive noun** shows ownership. Most plural nouns add an apostrophe after the -s to form the possessive (*chairs/chairs'*). Plurals that don't end in -s (*children, women*) add an apostrophe and -s (*children's, women's*) to show possession.

Practice

Write **S** above each singular common noun in the sentences below. Write **P** above each common plural noun. Circle each possessive noun.

1. Thomas Alva (Edison's) work probably makes him the greatest inventor of all time.
                              S   S   S

2. Called "the Wizard of Menlo Park," Edison patented 1,093 inventions.
                                                                    P

3. The (wizard's) work included improvements to existing devices.
        S   S   P   P

4. Edison improved the telephone, the typewriter, and motion pictures.
                        S   S   P

5. He brought the electric light into our homes.
                            S   P

6. He tried to develop good, reliable devices that would work without difficulty.
                                          P   S

7. Edison also wanted his inventions to be easy to fix.
                              P

8. Edison was interested in everything, including medicine.
                                                    S

9. His inventions changed the lives of millions of people.
        P   P   P   P

Strategies for Writers—Conventions & Skills Practice   Unit 2   **27**

Apply

Rewrite each sentence. Capitalize proper nouns. Add apostrophes to nouns that show ownership.

10. Edison was born on february 11, 1847, in milan, ohio. _____

Edison was born on February 11, 1847, in Milan, Ohio.

11. When he was just seven years old, Edisons family moved to michigan. _____

When he was just seven years old, Edison's family moved to Michigan.

12. He spent just three months at school in port huron. _____

He spent just three months at school in Port Huron.

13. With his mothers encouragement, edison read books such as the dictionary of sciences.

With his mother's encouragement, Edison read books such as The Dictionary of Sciences.

14. He earned money as a newsboy on the grand trunk railroad between port huron and detroit.

He earned money as a newsboy on the Grand Trunk Railroad between Port Huron and Detroit.

15. In new york, Edison noticed the tickers in stockbrokers offices often broke down.

In New York, Edison noticed the tickers in stockbrokers' offices often broke down.

16. Dr. samuel laws hired edison to repair and improve the stock tickers. _____

Dr. Samuel Laws hired Edison to repair and improve the stock tickers.

17. He used the money he earned to start his first laboratory in new jersey. _____

He used the money he earned to start his first laboratory in New Jersey.

18. Do you know edisons definition of "genius"? _____

Do you know Edison's definition of "genius"?

Personal, Compound, Possessive Pronouns

Learn

Maria Mitchell has many firsts to (her) credit in spite of the fact that, to a large extent, she educated **herself**.

Underline the boldfaced word that is made up of two smaller words.
Circle the boldfaced word that shows ownership.

To whom do the boldfaced words refer? _____Maria Mitchell_____

> A **pronoun** can take the place of a noun. Use the **personal pronouns** I, me, we, and us and the **compound personal pronouns** myself and ourselves to write about yourself. Use the personal pronouns she, her, it, he, him, you, they, and them and the compound personal pronouns herself, himself, itself, yourself, yourselves, and themselves to refer to other people and things. The **possessive pronouns** her, his, its, our, their, my, and your show possession.

Practice

Complete each sentence correctly by writing one of the pronouns in parentheses.

1. Maria Mitchell was known for _____her_____ work with planets. (her/herself)

2. Mitchell's father was an astronomer _____himself_____ . (himself/hisself)

3. When she was young, _____she_____ helped _____her_____ father in his work. (she/herself) (their/her)

4. In 1847, Mitchell discovered a new comet, which made _____her_____ famous. (her/them)

5. For this, the king of Denmark had _____his_____ country award _____her_____ a gold medal. (his/their) (herself/her)

6. The members of the American Academy of Arts and Sciences elected her the first woman to join _____their_____ group. (his/their)

7. _____She_____ served as a professor of astronomy at Vassar College. (Her/She)

8. When Mitchell was working by _____herself_____ , she found "Miss Mitchell's Comet" with just a two-inch telescope. (itself/herself)

Use the facts below to answer each question. Write a complete sentence, using at least one pronoun in each sentence.   Answers will vary. Possible responses appear below.

Maria Mitchell achieved the following:
- was mainly self-taught after leaving a "school for young ladies"
- first woman elected to the American Academy of Arts and Sciences
- first woman to have a comet named for her
- first woman elected to the American Philosophical Society (in 1869)
- awarded a gold medal by the king of Denmark
- served as a professor at Vassar College
- a founder of the American Association for the Advancement of Women

9. Where did Mitchell teach? _____

She taught at Vassar College.

10. What was "Miss Mitchell's Comet"? _____

It was a comet named for Maria Mitchell.

11. How did the American Academy of Arts and Sciences honor Mitchell? _____

They elected her to the academy.

12. What did the members of the American Philosophical Society have in common before 1869?

They were all men.

13. What did the king of Denmark do for Maria Mitchell? _____

He awarded her a gold medal.

14. What organization did Mitchell help found? _____

It was the American Association for the Advancement of Women.

15. Where did Mitchell get her professional education? _____

She was mainly self-taught.

Interrogative and Indefinite Pronouns

Learn

"**What** do we know about the weather?"

"(Everyone) talks about it, but (nobody) does anything about it."

Underline the boldfaced word that asks a question. Circle the boldfaced words that refer to a group of people or things.

> When the pronouns *who, whom, whose, which,* and *what* are used in questions, they are called **interrogative pronouns**. Use *who* as the subject of a clause or sentence. (*Who invented the wind scale?*) Use *whom* as a direct or indirect object or as the object of a preposition. (*For whom is the wind scale named?*) **Indefinite pronouns** refer to persons or things that are not identified as individuals. Indefinite pronouns include *all, anybody, both, either, anything, everyone, few, most, one, no one, several, nobody,* and *someone.*

Practice

Underline each interrogative pronoun. Circle each indefinite pronoun.

1. What is lightning? (Everyone) knows what it looks like, but few could tell you that it is a discharge of electricity from one cloud to another or between a cloud and the earth.

2. Which type of lightning appears as a jagged streak?

3. (Most) would probably call it forked lightning.

4. The fact that lightning is electricity was shown by whom? Ben Franklin proved it using a kite and a key.

5. Perhaps he shouldn't have tried it. (Some) who flew kites during storms have been electrocuted.

6. (Both) the ancient Greeks and Romans thought that lightning was a weapon of the gods.

7. Who knows how often lightning strikes the earth? There are about 100 strikes every second.

8. (Few) do any damage, but in the United States alone, about 100 people are killed each year. (Nobody) wants to be a victim, so it will help you to learn some safety measures.

Complete each sentence by writing a pronoun from the Word Bank. Remember to capitalize any word that begins a sentence. Some sentences have more than one correct answer.

Word Bank

some	what	which	no one	nobody
whom	someone	who	whose	many

9. ___What/Which___ kind of lightning appears as a glowing, fiery ball?

10. ___No one/Nobody___ knows why or how ball lightning happens.

11. A glowing light that may resemble ball lightning is named for ___whom___?

12. St. Elmo's fire might be seen by ___someone___ on a ship or an airplane.

13. ___Whose___ beliefs once included the idea that ringing church bells would keep away lightning?

14. ___Some/Many___ in England and America thought that ringing church bells would keep away lightning.

15. ___Who___ knows exactly how thunderclouds are formed?

16. ___Nobody/No one___ is sure, but ___many/some___ have theories.

17. ___What/Which___ kind of lightning appears as parallel streaks of light?

18. Ribbon lightning has probably been seen by ___someone___.

19. ___Some___ have seen dry lightning, lightning that occurs from a cloud that is not making rain.

20. ___Someone/Some___ might know that lightning helps nature by putting nitrogen in the ground for plants to use.

21. Surprisingly ___some/many___ have survived being struck by lightning.

22. ___Someone___ who stands under a tree during a thunderstorm is risking serious injury.

Action Verbs and Linking Verbs

Learn

The femur **is** our largest bone. We **can find** the smallest bone in the ear.

Which boldfaced verb shows action? _____can find_____

Which boldfaced verb links a noun with a phrase that describes the noun? _____is_____

> An **action verb** shows action. A **linking verb** does not show action. A linking verb connects the subject of a sentence to one or more words that describe or rename the subject. Linking verbs are usually forms of *be*. Common linking verbs include *am, is, are, was, were,* and *will be*. The verbs *become, seem, appear,* and *look* can also be used as linking verbs.

Practice

Circle each linking verb. Underline each action verb. Be sure to include helping verbs (*can, would, may, have*) when underlining action verbs.

1. There (are) a total of 27 bones just in one of your hands.

2. A simple movement of your fingers <u>requires</u> the use of 14 bones.

3. There (are) five bones in the palm of your hand.

4. You probably <u>can feel</u> all the bones in your thumb.

5. There (are) eight bones in the wrist.

6. The bodies of newborn babies <u>contain</u> an amazing 300 bones.

7. In time, some of those bones <u>grow</u> together.

8. These 300 bones eventually (become) 206 bones in an adult.

9. You <u>will find</u> the largest human bone in the leg.

10. A tall man's femur <u>can be</u> more than 20 inches long.

11. The smallest bone, the stirrup, (is) inside the ear.

**Apply**

Write each sentence. Add the kind of verb shown in parentheses. You may use words from the Word Bank or choose another verb. **Answers will vary. Possible responses appear below.**

Word Bank

contain	was	protect	are	find
is	give	were	fills	make

12. Bones (action) shape to the body. _____

     Bones give shape to the body.

13. The bones (linking) a support for our bodies. _____

     The bones are a support for our bodies.

14. In addition, bones (action) our vital organs. _____

     In addition, bones protect our vital organs.

15. You can (action) two kinds of bones in the human body. _____

     You can find two kinds of bones in the human body.

16. Long bones (action) up most of our arms and legs. _____

     Long bones make up most of our arms and legs.

17. The skull, spine, and pelvis (action) many short bones. _____

     The skull, spine, and pelvis contain many short bones.

18. The middle of a bone (linking) hollow. _____

     The middle of a bone is hollow.

19. Bone marrow (action) the hollow. _____

     Bone marrow fills the hollow.

20. Some bones (linking) closely attached to each other. _____

     Some bones are closely attached to each other.

21. Exercises (action) your bones stronger. Exercises make your bones stronger. _____

The Present, Past, and Future Tenses

Learn

Jerome (found) that there are more than one million kinds of animals. Scientists [classify] animals by certain characteristics. They probably **will discover** more kinds of animals in the future.

Underline the boldfaced words that tell about something that is going to happen.
Circle the boldfaced word that tells about something that has already happened. Draw a box around the boldfaced word that tells about something that happens regularly or is true now.

> A **present-tense verb** is used to indicate that something happens regularly or is true now. A **past-tense verb** tells about something that has already happened. Regular verbs form the past tense by adding -*ed*. Irregular verbs change their spelling in the past tense. A **future-tense verb** tells what is going to happen. Add the helping verb *will* to the present-tense form of a verb to form the future tense.

Practice

Underline each past-tense verb. Circle each present-tense verb. Draw a box around each future-tense verb.

1. Animals (live) in every part of the world, even Antarctica.

2. They (come) in many different sizes and shapes, including birds, insects, reptiles, and mammals.

3. Many kinds of animals became extinct during certain periods of time.

4. Thousands more species probably [will die] soon, in part because of human activities.

5. Dinosaurs disappeared about 65 million years ago.

6. Passenger pigeons existed in large numbers once.

7. They lost their habitat with the clearing of forests.

8. Hunters killed millions of nesting passenger pigeons as well.

9. Some zoos [will save] certain species from extinction through their programs.

10. Conservationists [will protect] certain animals in the wild.

Strategies for Writers—Conventions & Skills Practice **Unit 2**

Decide which tense of the verb in parentheses should be used in each sentence. Write the sentence using the correct tense of the verb. Add a helping verb if you need one.

11. Tamed animals _____ milk to their young and to many humans. (supply) _____

    Tamed animals supply milk to their young and to many humans.

12. Tibetans _____ yak milk. (drink) _____

    Tibetans drink yak milk.

13. You probably _____ about the use of milk from other animals. (know) _____

    You probably know about the use of milk from other animals.

14. People first _____ animal milk as food centuries ago. (use) _____

    People first used animal milk as food centuries ago.

15. We probably _____ animal milk for centuries to come. (enjoy) _____

    We probably will enjoy animal milk for centuries to come.

16. Domesticated animals _____ long ago to expect food from humans. (learn)

    Domesticated animals learned long ago to expect food from humans.

17. Wild animals, on the other hand, must often _____ great distances to find food. (travel)

    Wild animals, on the other hand, must often travel great distances to find food.

18. An arctic tern _____ incredible distances in its lifetime. (cover) _____

    An arctic tern covers incredible distances in its lifetime.

19. Whales normally _____ to cold waters in summer in order to feed. (go) _____

    Whales normally go to cold waters in summer in order to feed.

20. You _____ Galápagos penguins on the western island, where the water is cold. (find)

    You (can/will) find Galápagos penguins on the western island, where the water is cold.

The Present Perfect and Past Perfect Tenses

Learn

Inventions (have given) us many ways to live better. People **had used** fire for many years before the match was invented and made it easier to make fire.

Underline the boldfaced words that tell about actions that were completed in the past. Circle the boldfaced words that tell about an action that began in the past and continues today.

> The **present perfect** tense shows action that started in the past and was recently completed or is still happening. To form the present perfect tense, add the helping verb *has* or *have* to the past participle of a verb (*have given*). The **past perfect** tense shows action that was definitely completed in the past. To form the past perfect tense, add the helping verb *had* to the past participle of the verb (*had known*).

Practice

Underline the boldfaced verbs that are in the present perfect tense. Circle the boldfaced verbs that are in the past perfect tense. Draw a box around a verb that is neither. (**1.–12.**)

Often one invention **has led** to the need for another. For example, John Kay invented a flying shuttle weaving machine in 1733. This invention required another invention because it (**had allowed**) weavers to produce cloth faster than spinners could supply thread. The textile industry needed either more spinners or a faster spinning process. By the mid-1780s, other inventions (**had followed**) that made it possible for cloth to be produced quickly and cheaply.

Inventions in other industries **have produced** cheaper, better products. Inventions **have improved** bit by bit over the years. For example, look at the devices that **have appeared** recently to provide light. For generations people (**had relied**) on oil lamps and candles. Then gas and kerosene lamps **provided** the best light. We **have used** electric lights now for over a century. Neon signs **have added** color to city streets, and banks of lights **have made** night baseball possible. Inventions **have continued** to add both power and pleasure to our lives.

Write the complete sentences using the present perfect form or the past perfect form of the verb in parentheses. Use has or have with the past participle for the present perfect form. Use had and the past participle for the past perfect form.

13. People _____ many things over a period of nearly two million years. (invent)

 People have invented many things over a period of nearly two million years.

14. By about 3000 B.C., someone _____ the plow. (invented) _____

 By about 3000 B.C., someone had invented the plow.

15. By 1608, the telescope _____ new worlds to us. (open) _____

 By 1608, the telescope had opened new worlds to us.

16. By 1783, the balloon _____ our dreams of air travel. (encourage) _____

 By 1783, the balloon had encouraged our dreams of air travel.

17. Other inventions _____ communication. (improve) _____

 Other inventions have improved communication.

18. Some inventions _____ our health. (protect) _____

 Some inventions have protected our health.

19. Not all inventions _____ humankind. (help) _____

 Not all inventions have helped humankind.

20. By about 1350, the deadly cannon _____. (arrive) _____

 By about 1350, the deadly cannon had arrived.

21. The atomic bomb _____ our world. (change) _____

 The atomic bomb has changed our world.

The Present, Past, and Future Progressive Tenses

Learn

Today, more people **are driving** automobiles than ever before. Less than 100 years ago, people (**were laughing**) at these strange machines. Perhaps soon we ⬛**will be riding**⬛ in cars that are completely controlled by computers.

Underline the boldfaced verb phrase that tells about an action that is going on now. Circle the boldfaced verb phrase that tells about an action that was happening in the past. Draw a box around the verb phrase that tells about an action that will happen in the future.

> Verbs in **progressive tenses** show continuing action. To form the **present progressive** tense, add *am, is,* or *are* to the present participle of a verb. (*I am running.*) To form the **past progressive** tense, add *was* or *were* to the present participle. (*They were running.*) To form the **future progressive** tense, add *will be* to the present participle. (*You will be running.*)

Practice

Read each sentence. If the boldfaced verb is in a progressive tense, write **P** on the line. Write **X** if the boldfaced verb is not in a progressive tense.

1. When you study the history of automobiles, you **are learning** about some important scientific advances.   P _____

2. Pretend that you **are going** back in time to about 1770 when the first motor vehicle was invented.   P _____

3. That odd-looking device **used** steam to move its heavy frame.   X _____

4. By the 1830s, steam carriages **were carrying** passengers in England.   P _____

5. By 1885, two inventors **were building** a car engine powered by gasoline.   P _____

6. A few years later, William Morrison **developed** an electric-powered car.   X _____

7. By 1901, Ransom Olds **was producing** cars on a large scale.   P _____

8. Now manufacturers **are producing** cars on a gigantic scale.   P _____

9. Some **are manufacturing** cars that combine gas and electric engines.   P _____

Apply

Write each sentence. Add the boldfaced verb in parentheses. Write it in the tense indicated.

10. By 1900, the automobile _____ more appealing every year. (past progressive of **become**)

    By 1900, the automobile was becoming more appealing every year.

11. By 1901, two important events _____ even more to its appeal. (past progressive of **add**)

    By 1901, two important events were adding even more to its appeal.

12. Big oil fields in Texas _____ the market with oil. (past progressive of **flood**) _____

    Big oil fields in Texas were flooding the market with oil.

13. Soon gasoline prices _____ sharply. (past progressive of **drop**) _____

    Soon gasoline prices were dropping sharply.

14. Today, some people _____ about the supply of oil. (present progressive of **worry**) _____

    Today, some people are worrying about the supply of oil.

15. They think that soon we _____ out of oil. (future progressive of **run**) _____

    They think that soon we will be running out of oil.

16. Others _____ for the development of cleaner, more abundant fuels. (present progressive of **push**)

    Others are pushing for the development of cleaner, more abundant fuels.

17. They say cars _____ the air we breathe. (present progressive of **pollute**) _____

    They say cars are polluting the air we breathe.

18. Do you think we _____ this problem soon? (future progressive of **solve**) _____

    Do you think we will be solving this problem soon?

Adjectives and Adverbs

Learn

The **violent** windstorms that hit (suddenly) in Sudan, Africa, are called *haboobs*.

Underline the boldfaced word that describes a noun. Circle the boldfaced word that describes a verb.

> **Adjectives** describe nouns and pronouns. Some adjectives tell what kind. Others, like *many* and *five*, tell how many. The adjectives *this, that, these*, and *those* tell which one. These words are **demonstrative adjectives**. The articles *a, an*, and *the* are also adjectives. **Adverbs** describe verbs or adjectives. They tell how, when, where, or to what extent (how much). Many adverbs end in *-ly*. Other common adverbs are *fast, very, often, again, only, however, too, later, first, then, far, still*, and *now*.

Practice

Underline the boldfaced words that are adjectives. Circle the boldfaced words that are adverbs. Write **A** above each boldfaced adjective that is an article.

1. **A** **tropical** cyclone builds up over **warm** water in the tropics.

2. It may bring **intense** winds, **violent** thunder, and lightning.

3. It is (often) accompanied by **heavy** rains.

4. Hurricane is **another** name for **a** **tropical** cyclone formed in **the** West Indies or **the** eastern Pacific Ocean.

5. **The** **outer** winds of hurricanes move (quickly).

6. They blow over **seventy** miles an hour as they whirl around **the** eye.

7. **The** wind in **the** eye is **slower**.

8. **That** wind blows (only) **fifteen** miles per hour.

9. (Sometimes) **a** hurricane also produces **a** tornado.

10. **Tiny** **Australian** **tropical** cyclones are called willy-willies.

Rewrite each sentence. Add an adjective or an adverb. You may choose words from the Word Bank or use your own. **Answers will vary. Possible responses appear below.**

Word Bank

more	inward	cold-core	Northern
warm	warm-core	sometimes	lowest

11. In a cyclone, the winds spiral _____ toward the center. _____

In a cyclone, the winds spiral inward toward the center.

12. The center has the _____ atmospheric pressure, lower than the outer wind area.

The center has the lowest atmospheric pressure, lower than the outer wind area.

13. In the _____ Hemisphere, the winds blow counterclockwise. _____

In the Northern Hemisphere, the winds blow counterclockwise.

14. Cyclones are _____ called hurricanes. _____

Cyclones are sometimes called hurricanes.

15. Cyclones that are warmer at the core than near the edges are called _____ cyclones.

Cyclones that are warmer at the core than near the edges are called warm-core cyclones.

16. They often occur over very _____ land areas. _____

They often occur over very warm land areas.

17. Cyclones that are coldest near the center are called _____ cyclones. _____

Cyclones that are coldest near the center are called cold-core cyclones.

18. These cyclones may be very deep and are _____ intense several thousand feet in the air.

These cyclones may be very deep and are more intense several thousand feet in the air.

Prepositions and Interjections

Learn

Wow! You can add **with** an abacus.

Which boldfaced word shows a relationship between two words? _____ with _____

Which boldfaced word expresses emotion? _____ Wow _____

> A **preposition** shows a relationship between one word in a sentence and the noun or pronoun that follows the preposition. This noun or pronoun is called the **object of the preposition**. Common prepositions include *in, of, by, for,* and *into*. The preposition, the object of the preposition, and the words between them make a **prepositional phrase**. An **interjection** expresses emotion. *Ouch, oh, hey, hooray,* and *wow* are common interjections.

Practice

Underline the prepositional phrases. Then circle the preposition and its object. (Some sentences have more than one prepositional phrase.) Draw a box around each interjection.

1. Prehistoric people probably counted on their fingers.

2. They would record the number of sheep in a field. They might use a pebble for each animal.

3. Even then, geometry was needed for shaping clay into pottery.

4. Wow! We could learn about geometry from ancient cups and bowls.

5. The mathematicians of ancient Egypt used a decimal system.

6. They planned huge pyramids with complex calculations.

7. The ancient Babylonians developed a number system based on 60.

8. Oh! Did you know that we still measure time with such a system?

9. Hey! Sixty shows up in our minutes and seconds.

10. Exploring pure mathematics was first done by ancient Greek scholars.

11. Euclid explained an entire geometry system in one book.

Write each sentence. Add one or more prepositional phrases from the Word Bank.

Word Bank

in books and magazines   between two similar things

with Hindu-Arabic numerals   throughout history

with pi   of a circle's circumference

of the universe   of the printing press

12. A ratio is the relationship _____. _____

A ratio is the relationship between two similar things.

13. The ratio _____ to its diameter is called pi. _____

The ratio of a circle's circumference to its diameter is called pi.

14. If you know a circle's diameter, you can calculate its circumference _____.

If you know a circle's diameter, you can calculate its circumference with pi.

15. Roman numerals were gradually replaced _____. _____

Roman numerals were gradually replaced with Hindu-Arabic numerals.

16. Scientific knowledge spread rapidly after the invention _____. _____

Scientific knowledge spread rapidly after the invention of the printing press.

17. Copernicus published a book claiming that the sun, not Earth, was the center _____.

Copernicus published a book claiming that the sun, not Earth, was the center of the universe.

18. Today, scientists and mathematicians still publish their findings _____. _____

Today, scientists and mathematicians still publish their findings in books and magazines.

Coordinating and Subordinating Conjunctions

Learn

Among present-day animals, there is a clear difference between cold-blooded animals **and** warm-blooded animals. Scientists have long thought that dinosaurs were cold-blooded animals like lizards and fish, **but** some have begun to challenge that opinion. **If** dinosaurs were warm-blooded animals, some old ideas about them would have to change.

Which boldfaced word connects two nouns? _____ **and**

Which boldfaced word links two independent clauses? _____ **but**

Which boldfaced word begins a dependent clause? _____ **If**

> **Coordinating conjunctions** (*and, but, or*) connect words or groups of words (including independent clauses) of equal importance. **Subordinating conjunctions**, such as *although, because, since, so, if, that,* and *before,* connect a dependent clause with an independent clause. Subordinating conjunctions are used at the beginning of dependent clauses.

Practice

Circle each coordinating conjunction. Underline each subordinating conjunction.

1. Cold-blooded animals rely on their surroundings to regulate their body temperature, (but) warm-blooded animals regulate their own body temperature.

2. <u>Since</u> dinosaurs were considered to be reptiles, they were thought to be cold-blooded.

3. Cold-blooded animals, like lizards (or) frogs, grow slowly (and) tend to be inactive.

4. <u>Because</u> dinosaurs grew quickly, John Ostrom (and) Robert Baaker challenged the theory that dinosaurs were cold-blooded.

5. Cold-blooded animals cannot keep their body at a constant temperature, (but) warm-blooded animals can maintain a body temperature.

6. <u>Although</u> no living dinosaur is available, a variety of dinosaur bones have been found.

7. Later scientists, Reese Barrick (and) Bill Showers, looked for clues in bone structures.

8. They found <u>that</u> dinosaur bones are much like those of warm-blooded animals.

Apply

Use a conjunction from the Word Bank to complete each sentence. If the conjunction begins a sentence, be sure to capitalize it. You may use some words more than once.

Word Bank

so	although	because	and	or	but	since	if

9. One theory holds that dinosaurs grew quickly, like most warm-blooded animals, _____and_____ some baby dinosaurs grew so much while still in the nest.

10. _____Although_____ the leatherback sea turtle is cold-blooded, it keeps an almost constant body temperature.

11. _____Because/Since_____ some dinosaurs walked upright, more and more scientists believe that some dinosaurs were warm-blooded.

12. The size _____and_____ weight of some dinosaurs suggest that they were cold-blooded.

13. _____If_____ warm-blooded animals like the elephant have trouble keeping cool, the dinosaur would have had worse problems.

14. The debate over whether dinosaurs were warm-blooded _____or_____ cold-blooded will not be settled soon.

15. Taking a dinosaur's temperature is impossible _____because_____ none are still alive.

16. Yes, dinosaurs are extinct, _____but_____ we know an amazing amount about them.

17. However, _____since/because_____ the evidence goes in both directions, it is still difficult to put dinosaurs neatly into one category _____or_____ the other.

18. There is even more that we don't know, _____and_____ scientists will continue to debate the matter.

Passed and *Past*

Learn

The scientists flew to Egypt to study **past** civilizations. Their plane **passed** over the Sahara Desert.

Which boldfaced word means "existing at an earlier time"? _____ past _____

Which boldfaced word is the past tense of "pass"? _____ passed _____

> The words **passed** and **past** sound alike but have different spellings and meanings. *Passed* is the past-tense form of the verb *pass*, meaning "to go" or "to move by." *Past* is an adjective meaning "having existed or occurred at an earlier time" or a noun meaning "the time before the present."

Practice

Read these sentences. Underline the word in parentheses to complete each sentence correctly.

1. For hours, our plane (passed/past) over the barren sand of the Sahara Desert.

2. In the distant (passed/past), this parched desert was a rich grassland.

3. Scientists have found evidence of (passed/past) civilizations in the sands of the Sahara.

4. Travelers (passed/past) by stone tools and carvings, not knowing they came from ancient cultures.

5. In ancient times, raiders from Libya (passed/past) through the desert to attack Egypt.

6. Around the time of the Roman Empire, people (passed/past) over the desert on camels.

7. Desert tribes demanded tolls from caravans that (passed/past) through the desert.

8. In the (passed/past), nothing grew in the desert.

9. Thanks to irrigation, that time has (passed/past).

10. Some springs form an oasis, which thirsty travelers rarely (passed/past) without stopping.

11. These travelers may have (passed/past) the time watching whirls of dust, called waltzing jinns.

12. Often ten years will have (passed/past) before any rain falls.

**Apply**

Rewrite each sentence, adding **passed** or **past** to complete the sentence correctly.

13. We _____ people herding goats and sheep on the edge of the desert, where some rain falls.

    We passed people herding goats and sheep on the edge of the desert, where some rain falls.

14. Like _____ generations, these nomads move from place to place after all the grass is eaten.

    Like past generations, these nomads move from place to place after all the grass is eaten.

15. Drinking water is _____ carefully so as not to spill a precious drop.

    Drinking water is passed carefully so as not to spill a precious drop.

16. For centuries, caravans _____ over ground containing valuable resources.

    For centuries, caravans passed over ground containing valuable resources.

17. After World War II, the French found gas and oil that _____ explorers had ignored.

    After World War II, the French found gas and oil that past explorers had ignored.

18. Soon travelers _____ through the desert on asphalt roads.

    Soon travelers passed through the desert on asphalt roads.

19. By 1960, oil production in Algeria had _____ all estimates.

    By 1960, oil production in Algeria had passed all estimates.

20. The modern Sahara bears little resemblance to its forbidding _____.

    The modern Sahara bears little resemblance to its forbidding past.

Steel and *Steal*

Learn

The **steel** doors of the safe made it impossible for anyone to **steal** the money inside.

Which boldfaced word means "a type of metal"? _____steel_____

Which boldfaced word means "to take without permission"? _____steal_____

> The words **steel** and **steal** sound the same but have different meanings and spellings. *Steel* is a noun and means "a type of strong metal" or an adjective meaning "made of steel." *Steal* is a verb and means "to take without permission" or "to get or enjoy secretly."

Practice

Underline the word in parentheses that correctly completes each sentence.

1. Knives of the finest (steal/<u>steel</u>) are manufactured in Sheffield, England.

2. Competitors would like to (<u>steal</u>/steel) the secret for making such fine items.

3. The City Museum has a collection of (steal/<u>steel</u>) cutlery dating from the 16th century.

4. Residents of Sheffield often pop into the museum to (<u>steal</u>/steel) a quick look at their history.

5. Sheffield University has a school devoted to the study of (steal/<u>steel</u>) and metallurgy.

6. Part of Sheffield's secret for making blades would be hard to (<u>steal</u>/steel).

7. Their famous (steal/<u>steel</u>) is made from local iron and ground with sandstone from the area.

8. Without the local coalfield, it would not have become the home for such fine (steal/<u>steel</u>) products.

9. No one has been able to (<u>steal</u>/steel) Sheffield's name in fine (steal/<u>steel</u>) for six hundred years.

10. In 1865, Henry Bessemer invented a way to make (steal/<u>steel</u>) inexpensively.

11. His plant in Sheffield soon was producing large quantities of (steal/<u>steel</u>).

12. Do you think people from other areas tried to (<u>steal</u>/steel) his secret?

Strategies for Writers—Conventions & Skills Practice   **Unit 3**   **49**

Rewrite each sentence, adding **steal** or **steel** to complete the sentence correctly. If the word begins a sentence, remember to capitalize it.

13. It is hard to imagine a world without (steal/steel). _____

It is hard to imagine a world without steel.

14. (Steal/Steel) is found in cars, trains, cameras, tools, electrical equipment, and farm machinery.

Steel is found in cars, trains, cameras, tools, electrical equipment, and farm machinery.

15. Modern buildings depend on (steal/steel) beams to provide the strength needed for skyscrapers.

Modern buildings depend on steel beams to provide the strength needed for skyscrapers.

16. In the late 19th century, Germany developed a huge (steal/steel) industry using the coal of the Ruhr basin.

In the late 19th century, Germany developed a huge steel industry using the coal of the Ruhr basin.

17. In the 1930s, the United States was able to (steal/steel) some of the (steal/steel) business from Germany and England.

In the 1930s, the United States was able to steal some of the steel business from Germany and England.

18. In the 1980s, Japan and Korea were able to produce less-expensive (steal/steel).

In the 1980s, Japan and Korea were able to produce less-expensive steel.

Here and *Hear*

Learn

If we sit **here,** we should be able to **hear** the music clearly.

Which boldfaced word means "at this time or place"? _____ here

Which boldfaced word means "to receive sound through the ears"? _____ hear

> **Here** and **hear** sound the same but are spelled differently and have different meanings. *Here* is an adverb meaning "at this time or place," or a noun meaning "this place." *Hear* is a verb meaning "to be aware of" or "to receive through the ears."

Practice

Circle the word in parentheses that correctly completes each sentence.

1. (Hear/**Here**) in the U.S., immigrant traditions can be heard in a variety of folk songs.

2. If you travel to certain communities, you may (**hear**/here) some of these songs.

3. European immigrants arriving (hear/**here**) often brought their folk songs and music with them.

4. Some are still sung (hear/**here**) even though they have disappeared in Europe.

5. The banjo songs you (**hear**/here) in the U.S. probably were brought (hear/**here**) from Africa.

6. The bagpipes you (**hear**/here) on special occasions have an unknown origin.

7. The yodeling cowboy's music somehow got (hear/**here**) from the Alpine regions of Europe.

8. You can easily (**hear**/here) the unique sound of the zither in some Russian folk music.

9. You can (**hear**/here) lively dance tunes in Irish folk songs.

10. Jazz was born (hear/**here**), and people come from all over the world to (**hear**/here) it.

11. You will usually (**hear**/here) small cymbals and drums accompanying Asian vocal folk music.

12. It is not unusual to (**hear**/here) folk music reflected in the works of classical composers.

Rewrite each sentence, adding **here** or **hear** to complete the sentence correctly. If the word begins a sentence, remember to capitalize it.

13. Folk songs are not always written down, so you may not _____ them the same way twice.

Folk songs are not always written down, so you may not hear them the same way twice.

_____

14. _____ in the U.S., folk songs often told stories of disasters or other events.

Here in the U.S., folk songs often told stories of disasters or other events.

_____

15. Each generation might _____ a somewhat different version of the story.

Each generation might hear a somewhat different version of the story.

_____

16. Some songs got _____ when workers brought them from the mines and fields.

Some songs got here when workers brought them from the mines and fields.

_____

17. When they could _____ these songs, they forgot about the hard work they had to do.

When they could hear these songs, they forgot about the hard work they had to do.

_____

18. _____, as in most countries of the world, folk music is an important part of festivals.

Here, as in most countries of the world, folk music is an important part of festivals.

_____

19. Thanks to the work of music historians, we will be able to _____ old folk songs.

Thanks to the work of music historians, we will be able to hear old folk songs.

_____

20. They have traveled _____ and there to _____ the music and words and record them.

They have traveled here and there to hear the music and words and record them.

_____

Being Careful with *Go*, *Went*, and *Like*

Learn

Greg **went,** "Antarctica is the coldest and iciest region in the world."
"Is it colder than the North Pole?" (asked) Anita.
Rita **was like,** "Brrrr!"

Circle the boldfaced word that correctly shows someone is speaking.

> **Go** and **went** mean "move(d) from place to place." **Is like** means "resembles something." Use verbs such as *say, ask, answer, shout,* and *whisper* to indicate that someone is speaking. Avoid using go, *goes, went,* or *is like* to mean "says."

Practice

Cross out each incorrect use of *go, went,* or *like.* Circle each correct use of these words. (**1.–12.**)

After the students watched a film about Antarctica, they all (went) outside. They were eager to talk more about what they saw.

Rita we~~n~~t, "Isn't it something that we don't know for certain who first saw Antarctica?"

Then Greg go~~e~~s, "It's interesting to me that so many animals live there, at least in the water."

Anita we~~n~~t, "There are li~~k~~e only a few insects and small plants."

Rita w~~a~~s li~~k~~e, "Some of the plants are algae that look (like) pink or green snow."

Anita said, "The penguins are the cutest animals. They look (like) little people wearing tuxedos."

Greg we~~n~~t, "It sure was a great film about the South Pole."

Rita go~~e~~s, "The race between Scott and Amundsen was very dramatic."

Anita w~~a~~s li~~k~~e, "It was sad that all five men in Scott's party died."

Greg we~~n~~t, "Yes, but they made it to the pole."

Apply

Rewrite each sentence to eliminate any incorrect expressions. There is more than one way to rewrite each sentence. **Possible responses appear below.**

13. Greg was like, "Does any land at all show up in Antarctica?" _____

Greg asked, "Does any land at all show up in Antarctica?"

14. Anita went, "You can see a few mountain peaks and, like, a few other bare rocky areas."

Anita answered, "You can see a few mountain peaks and a few other bare rocky areas."

15. Rita goes, "I think the film said 98 percent of the continent is covered with ice and snow."

Rita added, "I think the film said 98 percent of the continent is covered with ice and snow."

16. Greg went, "What would the land look like if we could see it?" _____

Greg asked, "What would the land look like if we could see it?"

17. Rita was like, "It is a lot like the landforms on the other continents." _____

Rita replied, "It is a lot like the landforms on the other continents."

18. Anita goes, "We can see the highest mountain peaks." _____

Anita said, "We can see the highest mountain peaks."

19. Greg goes, "It's hard to imagine that it was once ice free." _____

Greg stated, "It's hard to imagine that it was once ice free."

20. Rita went, "They've found fossils of trees and dinosaurs." _____

Rita commented, "They've found fossils of trees and dinosaurs."

21. Greg goes, "Then glaciers started forming, like, about 30 million years ago."

Greg continued, "Then glaciers started forming about 30 million years ago."

22. Anita was like, "Ice still covers Greenland, too." _____

Anita explained, "Ice still covers Greenland, too."

Good and *Well*

Learn

I'm reading a **good** book about furniture making. If furniture is built **well,** it will last a long time.

Which boldfaced word tells more about a noun? _____ good _____

Which boldfaced word tells more about a verb? _____ well _____

> **Good** is an adjective. Use it to describe a noun. **Well** is an adverb. Use it to tell more about a verb. You can also use *well* as an adjective to mean "healthy."

Practice

Circle the word being described by the word in parentheses. Is it a noun or a verb? Underline the word in parentheses that correctly completes each sentence.

1. Some think of art as being a (good/well) (painting).

2. Others think of art as anything that is (done) (good/well).

3. A craftsperson may feel something that is beautiful and (does) a job (good/well) qualifies as art.

4. Colonial American quilts are not only (made) (good/well), they often give charming glimpses of life in early America.

5. Pottery is a (good/well) (example) of how a necessary object can become a work of art.

6. The Egyptians made glazed pottery, and we see their (good/well) (works) in museums.

7. The early Cretans made pottery that (worked) (good/well) and delighted the eye.

8. The Cretans influenced the Greeks, and the Greeks (learned) their lessons (good/well).

9. Weavers were another group whose craft was (done) so (good/well) that it became art.

10. There is a (good/well) (chance) that textile weaving developed from basket weaving.

11. Ancient wall paintings offer (good/well) (evidence) of this.

12. The ancient Chinese made silk thread that was put to (good/well) (use) by the weavers.

13. Navajo rugs are examples of (weaving) that looks (good/well) and (wears) (good/well).

14. People in every culture have valued the (good/well) (work) of their craftspeople.

Read the paragraph below. Then complete items **15.–20.** You may also use your own experience and knowledge in completing the exercise. **Answers will vary.**

Until the 1800s, almost everything that people used had to be made or crafted by hand. Craftspeople made cloth, tools, toys, shelters, furniture, pottery, and nearly everything used around the home. These items were often painstakingly carved, shaped, and fitted. A chair may have taken weeks to create, beginning with the selection of the wood from a mature tree. The result was a chair that was comfortable for the body as well as attractive to the eye.

15. Write a sentence about cloth making using the word *good*.

_____

_____

16. Write a sentence about cloth making using the word *well*.

_____

_____

17. Write a sentence about pottery using the word *good*.

_____

_____

18. Write a sentence about pottery using the word *well*.

_____

_____

19. Write a sentence about toolmaking using the word *good*.

_____

_____

20. Write a sentence about toolmaking using the word *well*.

_____

_____

Doesn't and *Don't*

Learn

We **don't** know who created most folk songs. It really **doesn't** matter, though, because folk songs often change each time they are performed.

Which boldfaced word is used with a singular subject? _____ doesn't _____

Which boldfaced word is used with a plural subject? _____ don't _____

> Use the contraction **doesn't** with singular subjects, including *he, she,* and *it.* Use the contraction **don't** with plural subjects, including *we* and *they.* Also use *don't* with *I* and *you.*

Practice

Circle the word in parentheses that correctly completes each sentence.

1. Most people in the world (doesn't/**don't**) get through the day without hearing some music.

2. There is hardly a community that (**doesn't**/don't) enjoy and create music.

3. We (doesn't/**don't**) know for sure how long humans have been making music.

4. Some say that people started singing as soon as they developed language. That seems like a pretty good guess, (**doesn't**/don't) it?

5. We (doesn't/**don't**) know how they did it, but ancient people learned to make flutes from bones.

6. Ancient people used music in religious ceremonies. Some things (doesn't/**don't**) change much.

7. Folk music takes many forms. The music of one culture (**doesn't**/don't) always sound like the music of another culture.

8. Folk music includes love songs and songs about real events. It (**doesn't**/don't) include symphonies, operas, or ballet.

9. Folk music usually (**doesn't**/don't) develop over a short period of time.

10. Folk songs change as they are passed through generations. However, it (**doesn't**/don't) take long to learn the popular tunes.

Apply

Rewrite each sentence, adding **doesn't** or **don't** to complete the sentence correctly.

11. Folk music _____ take form overnight. _____

Folk music doesn't take form overnight.

12. One person will turn a story into a song, but the changes _____ end there.

One person will turn a story into a song, but the changes don't end there.

13. Through time, several accounts may develop, but the essential story _____ change.

Through time, several accounts may develop, but the essential story doesn't change.

14. Although different versions of the story may develop, the melody _____ change.

Although different versions of the story may develop, the melody doesn't change.

15. Most American folk songs have a repeating chorus, but some choruses _____ use real words.

Most American folk songs have a repeating chorus, but some choruses don't use real words.

16. These choruses use syllables that _____ have any meaning. _____

These choruses use syllables that don't have any meaning.

17. The chorus of a folk song _____ change, although the verses change to tell the story.

The chorus of a folk song doesn't change, although the verses change to tell the story.

18. A folk song _____ always requires musical instruments, but they can add to the listeners' pleasure.

A folk song doesn't always require musical instruments, but they can add to the listeners' pleasure.

Threw and *Through*

Learn

I **threw** the ball as hard as I could, but the batter hit the ball **through** my legs.

Underline the boldfaced word that is the past tense of "throw."
Circle the boldfaced word that means "between."

> **Threw** and **through** sound alike but are spelled differently and have different meanings. *Threw* is the past tense of "throw." *Through* is a preposition meaning "in one side and out the other," "between," or "by way of." It can also be an adverb meaning "from one end to another," or an adjective meaning "finished."

Practice

Circle the word in parentheses that correctly completes each sentence.

1. When people are (threw/**through**) with their work, they often enjoy playing games.

2. Native American boys went (threw/**through**) the woods pretending to be hunters or warriors.

3. Girls wound string-like fibers (threw/**through**) their fingers to make a cat's cradle.

4. In one game, the players (**threw**/through) a long stick to see who could get it over a river.

5. In a game similar to modern football, women often kicked or (**threw**/through) a small ball across a field.

6. In one game, the players carried or (**threw**/through) a ball back and forth toward an opponent's goal.

7. (Threw/**Through**) the years, this game evolved into the modern sport of lacrosse.

8. Some northern tribes played a game in which players (**threw**/through) peach seeds into a bowl.

9. As games became popular, they spread (threw/**through**) the camp.

10. (Threw/**Through**) hours of training, many Native Americans became experts at such games.

Rewrite each sentence, adding **threw** or **through** to complete the sentence correctly. If the word begins a sentence, be sure to capitalize it.

11. The Olympic Games hope to promote peace between the nations _____ athletic competition.

The Olympic Games hope to promote peace between nations through athletic competition.

_____

12. In the first Olympic Games, contestants _____ spears to test their strength and accuracy.

In the first Olympic Games, contestants threw spears to test their strength and accuracy.

_____

13. _____ the years, this event has evolved into the javelin throw. _____

Through the years, this event has evolved into the javelin throw.

_____

14. The Olympic Games were abolished in A.D. 394, but _____ a successful campaign by Baron Pierre de Coubertin, they were revived in 1896.

The Olympic Games were abolished in A.D. 349, but through a successful campaign by

Baron Pierre de Coubertin, they were revived in 1896.

_____

15. In the early games, spectators often _____ flowers and olive branches on victorious athletes.

In the early games, spectators often threw flowers and olive branches on victorious athletes.

_____

16. Winners marched _____ a grove of olive trees, followed by a musician playing a flute.

Winners marched through a grove of olive trees, followed by a musician playing a flute.

_____

17. The games have gone _____ many changes in the nearly 2,000 years since they began.

The games have gone through many changes in the nearly 2,000 years since they began.

_____

18. It is _____ the efforts of the athletes, however, that the Olympics have survived.

It is through the efforts of the athletes, however, that the Olympics have survived.

_____

Cent, Sent, Scent

Learn

The **scent** of freshly baked bread **sent** crowds of people to the bakery shop.
The baker would sell a loaf for five dollars, and she would not take a **cent** less.

Which boldfaced word means "a distinct, usually pleasing odor"? _____ scent _____

Which boldfaced word is the past tense and past participle of **send**? _____ sent _____

Which boldfaced word means "coin" or "a small amount of money"? _____ cent _____

> The words **scent, sent,** and **cent** sound the same but have different meanings and spellings. *Scent* is a noun that means "a distinct, usually pleasing odor." *Sent* is the past tense and past participle of *send. Cent* is a noun meaning "a penny" or "a small amount of money."

Practice

Circle the word in parentheses that correctly completes each sentence.

1. The ancient Egyptians were probably the first to extract a (scent/sent/cent) from flowers.

2. The Greeks learned how to create pleasing (scents/cents) from the Egyptians.

3. The Romans took perfumed (scents/cents) to France and England.

4. Early perfumes were expensive, but now a (scent/sent/cent) can cost just a few (scents/cents).

5. In the 1500s, the (scents/cents) of France became the most popular in the world.

6. French kings (scent/sent/cent) servants to perfume the palace walls and furniture.

7. The people of Ireland created (scents/cents) from lavender.

8. However, one (scent/sent/cent) will not buy a fine perfume today.

9. It takes a carefully measured combination of ingredients to produce a desired (scent/sent/cent).

10. Today there are hundreds of perfumes costing from a few (scents/cents) to thousands of dollars.

Apply

Follow the directions to write a sentence. **Answers will vary.**

11. Use *scent* in a sentence about a ceremony. _____

_____

12. Use *cent* in a sentence about the history of perfume. _____

_____

13. Use *sent* in a sentence about a present you gave someone. _____

_____

14. Use *scent* in a sentence about a bakery. _____

_____

15. Use *cent* in a sentence about an expensive soap or bath oil. _____

_____

16. Use *sent* in a sentence about shipping precious items long distances.

_____

_____

17. Use *scent* in a sentence about a great meal you had. _____

_____

18. Use *sent* in a sentence about a bad smell. _____

_____

19. Use *cent* in a sentence about the price of something. _____

_____

20. Use *scent* in a sentence about an unusual custom. _____

_____

Leave and *Let; Rise* and *Raise*

Learn

"**Let** us play with your team," said Alisha.

"No. **Leave** us alone until we have finished this game," said José.

"What if we can **raise** enough players to make another team?" asked Alisha.

"Then we'll play your team. Who knows? You may **rise** up and beat us," said José.

Which boldfaced word means "go to a higher position"? _____ *rise*

Which boldfaced word means "allow"? _____ *let*

Which boldfaced word means "go away from"? _____ *leave*

Which boldfaced word means "collect"? _____ *raise*

> The verbs **leave** and **let** are often confused. *Leave* means "to let remain in place" or "to go away from." *Let* means "to allow." The verbs **rise** and **raise** are also often confused. *Rise* does not need a direct object. *Raise* must be followed by a direct object.

Practice

Circle the word in parentheses that correctly completes each sentence.

1. "(**Let**/Leave) me tell you what I have been reading about games," exclaimed Alisha.

2. "(**Let**/Leave) me guess," said José. "Games have been with us for thousands of years."

3. "Since you have (rose/**raised**) the subject," said Yi, "I know that games are played everywhere."

4. "A Chinese game (**rises**/raises) to my mind," said Yi. "Have you heard of mah-jongg?"

5. "(**Let**/Leave) me tell you about the Japanese game *go*," responded José.

6. "(**Let**/Leave) me think," said Alisha. "Isn't *go* a board game?"

7. "Let me (rise/**raise**) a question," interrupted José. "Don't all games fit into six categories?"

8. Alisha answered, "The six categories (let/**leave**) out games like jumping rope and Simon says."

Complete each sentence in your own words. Be sure to use **leave, let, rise,** and **raise** correctly. Remember to end the sentence with the correct punctuation. **Answers will vary.**

9. If the park supervisor lets us, _____

_____

10. We need equipment. I hope we can raise _____

_____

11. We will rise _____

_____

12. Perhaps we can leave _____

_____

13. Let me explain _____

_____

14. If I can rise _____

_____

15. Please raise _____

_____

16. After you leave _____

_____

17. Do not let _____

_____

18. Rise _____

_____

Irregular Verbs: *Fly, Run, Swim*

Learn

The Inca runners carried messages. A messenger **ran** from one village to the next.
They **ran** on very good roads, so they must have **ran̶ed** fast.

Cross out the boldfaced word that is used incorrectly.

> The verbs **fly, run,** and **swim** are **irregular**. You cannot make the past tense or the past participle of these verbs by adding *-ed*. These verbs have different forms.
>
> | Present Tense | Past Tense | Past Participle (With *have, has,* or *had*) |
> |---|---|---|
> | fly/flies | flew | flown |
> | run/runs | ran | run |
> | swim/swims | swam | swum |

Practice

Circle the correct word in parentheses.

1. People have (swam/**swum**) and (**run**/ran) for ages.

2. However, they have (flew/**flown**) only since the 1700s.

3. People have watched birds (**fly**/flew) for ages, too.

4. Before the 1700s, however, a human being had never (flew/**flown**).

5. In 1783, a man (fly/**flew**) above the earth in a hot air balloon.

6. Spectators stood in awe as they watched him (**fly**/flew) through the air.

7. People probably first (**swam**/swum) by imitating the ways animals move through the water.

8. Men (**swam**/swum) in international meets during the 1896 Olympic Games.

9. Before modern communication became available, special messengers (run/**ran**) great distances to deliver messages quickly.

10. The Greeks (run/**ran**) footraces at least 2,000 years ago.

Apply

Answer each question below. Use the correct form of *fly, run,* or *swim* in your answer.

11. When did someone fly for the first time?

_____

_____

12. What do you think the viewers of this first flight might have said?

_____

_____

13. How did early messengers get their messages from place to place?

_____

_____

14. What resulted from watching animals move through water?

_____

_____

15. What new event might you have seen at the 1896 Olympic Games?

_____

_____

16. How long have footraces been part of the Olympic Games?

_____

_____

17. What did someone do for the first time in a hot air balloon?

_____

_____

18. What might that person have said after he returned to the earth?

_____

_____

Subject and Object Pronouns

Learn

a. Mark Twain, one of the most popular American writers, often set his stories on or near the Mississippi River.

b. **He** sometimes used **them** to poke fun at society.

Which boldfaced word replaces *Mark Twain*? _____ He _____

Which boldfaced word replaces *stories*? _____ them _____

Which word is the subject of sentence **b.**? _____ He _____

> A pronoun can take the place of a subject or an object in a sentence. **Subject pronouns** include *I, he, she, we,* and *they*. **Object pronouns** can be used after an action verb or a preposition. Object pronouns include *me, him, her, us,* and *them*. The pronouns *it* and *you* can be either subjects or objects.

Practice

Underline each boldfaced word that is a subject pronoun. Circle each boldfaced word that is an object pronoun.

1. Mark Twain is one of my favorite authors. **He** used Mark Twain as a pen name. His real name was Samuel Langhorne Clemens.

2. **He** spent his youth in Hannibal, Missouri, a small town on the Mississippi River.

3. In 1859, when **he** was 24 years old, **he** became a riverboat pilot.

4. **It** was an important decision for **him**.

5. **It** was a job that paid well and taught **him** a lot about human nature.

6. **He** took his pen name from a riverboat term. **It** refers to water that is two fathoms deep (a depth of about 12 feet).

7. With time, riverboats became out-of-date. Eventually, **they** disappeared from the river.

8. Twain went to Nevada to be with his brother. **They** prospected for gold and silver, hoping it would make **them** rich.

Strategies for Writers—Conventions & Skills Practice   Unit 4

Rewrite each sentence. Replace each boldfaced word or phrase with a subject pronoun or an object pronoun.

9. Mark Twain published his first short story in 1865. **The story** was called "The Celebrated Jumping Frog of Calaveras County."

He published his first short story in 1865. It was called "The Celebrated Jumping Frog of Calaveras County."

_____

10. This story gave **Twain** an early taste for the type of writing that would make him famous.

It gave him an early taste for the type of writing that would make him famous.

_____

11. In 1870, **Mark Twain** married Olivia Langdon. _____

In 1870, he married Olivia Langdon.

12. Mark and Olivia had a son who died while still an infant. Three daughters were born to **Mark and Olivia** between 1872 and 1880.

They had a son who died while still an infant. Three daughters were born to them between 1872 and 1880.

_____

13. A book called The Gilded Age was published in 1873. **The Gilded Age** was Twain's first novel. **Twain** wrote it with Charles Dudley Warner.

A book called The Gilded Age was published in 1873. It was Twain's first novel. He wrote it with

Charles Dudley Warner.

_____

14. In 1876, **Twain** published The Adventures of Tom Sawyer.

In 1876, he published The Adventures of Tom Sawyer.

_____

15. People say his greatest work is The Adventures of Huckleberry Finn. **The Adventures of Huckleberry Finn** brought **Mark Twain** much critical acclaim.

They say his greatest work is The Adventures of Huckleberry Finn. It brought him much critical acclaim.

_____

Pronouns in Pairs

Learn

   a. Lorena and **me** read Emily Dickinson's poems.
   b. Mr. Chung told Lorena and **me** about this gifted poet.

If you remove "Lorena and" from each sentence, which sentence sounds correct? _____**b.**_____

> Use a **subject pronoun** in a compound subject. Use an **object pronoun** in a compound direct object, compound indirect object, or compound object of a preposition. If you are unsure which pronoun form to use, say the sentence to yourself without the other part of the compound. For example, "Lorena and me read Emily Dickinson's poems" becomes "Me read Emily Dickinson's poems." You can hear that *me* should be replaced with *I*.

Practice

Circle the correct pronoun in each pair. Write **S** if you chose a subject pronoun and **O** if you chose an object pronoun.

1. Mr. Chung asked Josh, Maria, Running Bear, and (I/**me**) to read several of Emily Dickinson's poems aloud.   O

2. Running Bear and (**I**/me) already knew some of her poems.   S

3. (**He**/Him) and Josh asked what we knew about her.   S

4. We explained to Josh and (he/**him**) that nobody knew very much. We knew that she was born in 1830.   O

5. Mr. Chung reminded Lorena and (I/**me**) that Emily Dickinson spent most of her time at home.   O

6. Lorena and (**I**/me) knew that she wrote over 1,700 poems.   S

7. (**She**/Her) and Maria added that most of Dickinson's poems were very short.   S

8. Maria and (**she**/her) have read a lot of them.   S

Rewrite each sentence. Replace each boldfaced noun with a pronoun.

9. **Lorena** and **Josh** agreed that Dickinson's poems can sometimes be hard to understand.

   She and he agreed that Dickinson's poems can sometimes be hard to understand.

   _____

10. Mr. Chung pointed out to Lorena and **Josh** that Dickinson's poetry is not like anyone else's.

    Mr. Chung pointed out to Lorena and him that Dickinson's poetry is not like anyone else's.

    _____

11. Running Bear told Josh and **Maria** that many of Dickinson's poems are concerned with a fleeting moment.

    Running Bear told Josh and her that many of Dickinson's poems are concerned with

    a fleeting moment.

    _____

12. **Running Bear** and Josh added that many of the poems are concerned with death.

    He and Josh added that many of the poems are concerned with death.

    _____

13. Mr. Chung told **Lorena** and me that Dickinson did not want to publish her poems.

    Mr. Chung told her and me that Dickinson did not want to publish her poems.

    _____

14. He told **the class** that at least ten poems were published during her lifetime.

    He told (us/them) that at least ten poems were published during her lifetime.

    _____

15. Maria and **Lorena** said they understood the poems were published without her permission.

    Maria and she said they understood the poems were published without her permission.

    _____

Pronoun Antecedents

Learn

William Shakespeare was a poet and a playwright. **He** is perhaps the greatest dramatist the world has ever known.

What noun does the boldfaced pronoun replace? _____William Shakespeare_____

> An **antecedent** is the word or phrase a pronoun refers to. The antecedent includes a noun. When you write a pronoun, be sure its antecedent is clear. Pronouns must **agree** with their antecedents. An antecedent and a pronoun agree when they have the same number (singular or plural) and gender (male, female, or neuter).

Practice

Circle the antecedent of each boldfaced pronoun.

1. (Shakespeare) was also a poet. **He** is considered one of the finest poets of the English language.

2. (People) everywhere have produced his plays. **They** have staged them over and over.

3. (Words) from Shakespeare's plays have become part of our everyday speech. **They** include the familiar phrases "fair play" and "catch cold."

4. (Shakespeare) also invented words. Scholars credit **him** with such words as *bump* and *lonely*.

5. Shakespeare's (plays) appeal to us. We see situations in **them** that we recognize.

6. The main reason is that (Shakespeare) understood human nature. **He** understood people.

7. His (characters) are unique human beings. **They** grapple with problems just as real people do.

8. Sometimes his (characters) succeed, and sometimes **they** don't.

9. (Shakespeare) wrote at least 37 plays. **He** wrote tragedies, comedies, and histories.

10. He was born in (Stratford-upon-Avon). **It** is about 75 miles northwest of London.

Apply

Write the pronoun that could replace or relate to each boldfaced word or phrase. If the pronoun begins a sentence, capitalize it.

11. He was baptized at **Holy Trinity church** in Stratford. _____Its_____ records show that he was baptized on April 26, 1564.

12. Shakespeare's parents were **John and Mary Arden Shakespeare**. William was the third of eight children born to _____them_____.

13. **Shakespeare's school** had classes almost all year. _____It_____ was strict and demanding.

14. **Shakespeare** must have spent a lot of time outdoors, because _____he_____ shows a love of nature in many of his poems.

15. In 1582, Shakespeare married **Anne Hathaway**. _____She_____ was eight years older than Shakespeare.

16. **Shakespeare** was only 18 years old at the time of _____his_____ marriage.

17. **Will and Anne** had their first child in 1583. _____They_____ named her Susanna.

18. Two years later, Anne gave birth to **twins**. Records show that _____they_____ were baptized on February 2, 1585.

19. Some scholars call **the period between 1585 to 1592** the lost years. _____It_____ is a time when there is no record of where Shakespeare lived or worked.

20. According to some scholars, **Shakespeare** may have been using this time to lay the foundation for _____his_____ career as a playwright.

21. He became a member of the **Lord Chamberlain's Men**. _____It_____ was a company of professional actors.

22. He wrote many of the characters in his plays with specific **actors** in mind. He would think about particular skills _____they_____ had.

23. The order in which **Shakespeare** wrote _____his_____ plays is uncertain.

24. You might enjoy reading ***The Shakespeare Stealer***. _____It_____ and _____its_____ sequel, *Shakespeare's Scribe*, are about a boy who joins Shakespeare's company.

Using *Who* or *Whom*

Learn

Willa Cather is an American author **who** became famous for her novels. _____ subject _____

Cather wrote about immigrant women for **whom** life was harsh. _____ object _____

Underline the clause and phrase that include *who* and *whom*. After each sentence, write whether *who* or *whom* is a subject or an object.

> Use **who** as the **subject** of a sentence or a clause. Use **whom** as the **object** of a verb or a preposition.

Practice

Decide whether the word in parentheses will be a subject or an object. Then circle the word in parentheses that completes each sentence correctly.

1. Willa Cather, (who/whom) was born in Virginia, moved to Nebraska at the age of 9.

2. Willa, for (who/whom) the green hills of Virginia were ideal, was surprised by the landscape of Red Cloud, Nebraska.

3. The family had moved because of her grandfather, (who/whom) believed that the climate would be healthier for the family.

4. Willa was schooled at home by her grandmother, (who/whom) taught her from the family's many books.

5. Part of her education came from the neighbors (who/whom) she rode out to visit.

6. These are the people from (who/whom) she learned much about life on the prairie.

7. Willa admired these hard-working people, some of (who/whom) showed up in her novels and stories.

8. She sometimes visited her German neighbors, (who/whom) had a grove of catalpa trees.

9. When she went to Red Cloud High School, she made two adult friends. One was Mrs. Minor, from (who/whom) she acquired a love of music.

10. When she left Red Cloud for college, Willa left behind the people (who/whom) she had known on the Nebraska prairie.

Apply

Rewrite each sentence. Add *who* or *whom* to complete the sentence correctly.

11. Willa Cather wrote about people _____ she had known in Nebraska. _____

Willa Cather wrote about people whom she had known in Nebraska.

12. These pioneers, _____ managed to survive on the rugged prairie, earned her admiration.

These pioneers, who managed to survive on the rugged prairie, earned her admiration.

13. The Cather family, _____ had lived in Virginia, moved near Red Cloud, Nebraska.

The Cather family, who had lived in Virginia, moved near Red Cloud, Nebraska.

14. As a girl, Cather listened to stories told by immigrant women, many of _____ were from Sweden or Bohemia.

As a girl, Cather listened to stories told by immigrant women, many of whom were from Sweden

or Bohemia.

15. _____ could have guessed that such modest beginnings would lead to worldwide fame?

Who could have guessed that such modest beginnings would lead to worldwide fame?

16. Her characters, _____ readers found irresistible, won her a large audience.

Her characters, whom readers found irresistible, won her a large audience.

17. Living quietly in New York City, Cather, _____ avoided public appearances, devoted herself to writing and traveling.

Living quietly in New York City, Cather, who avoided public appearances, devoted herself to writing

and traveling.

Making the Subject and Verb Agree

Learn

The (entries) in a **dictionary** give many facts about words.

Circle the boldfaced noun above that is the simple subject.

Is the noun singular or plural? _____ plural _____
Underline the verb.

> The **subject** and its **verb must agree**. Add -s or -es to a regular verb in the present tense when the subject is a singular noun or *he, she,* or *it*. Do not add -s or -es to a regular verb in the present tense when the subject is a plural noun or *I, you, we,* or *they*. Be sure that the verb agrees with its subject and not with the object of a preposition that comes before the verb.

Practice

Circle the simple subject in each sentence. Decide whether the subject is singular or plural. Then underline the correct form of each verb in parentheses. Make sure the subject and verb agree.

1. (Words) in most dictionaries (appear/appears) in alphabetical order.

2. The (dictionaries) in your school (contain/contains) words you read or need to write.

3. After a word, (you) often (find/finds) its pronunciation and part of speech.

4. To save space, a (dictionary) with many words (use/uses) abbreviations for the parts of speech.

5. Many (entries) in the dictionary (include/includes) several definitions.

6. One (type) of definition (place/places) a word in a particular category.

7. For example, one (definition) for *jungle* (begin/begins) "an area of land."

8. Next, a (definition) of this type (tell/tells) how a jungle differs from other areas of land.

9. A (phrase) such as "with dense tropical trees and plants" (follow/follows) the initial words.

10. Larger (dictionaries) of the English language (present/presents) the history of the word.

Rewrite each sentence. Add a verb from the Word Bank or another verb to complete each sentence correctly. **Answers may vary. Possible responses appear below.**

Word Bank

mean/means	depend/depends	define/defines
earn/earns	work/works	use/uses
give/gives	take/takes	name/names

11. To define words we sometimes _____ examples. _____

    To define words we sometimes give examples.

12. To define *red*, this dictionary _____ several things that are red. _____

    To define *red*, this dictionary names several things that are red.

13. Dictionaries today _____ a word based on how people use it. _____

    Dictionaries today define a word based on how people use it.

14. For example, today *presently* _____ *at present* as well as *soon*. _____

    For example, today *presently* means *at present* as well as *soon*.

15. A slang term with several meanings rarely _____ easy acceptance in a dictionary.

    A slang term with several meanings rarely earns easy acceptance in a dictionary.

16. New words often _____ years to be accepted by dictionary editors. _____

    New words often take years to be accepted by dictionary editors.

Forms of *Be*

Learn

a. Our vocabulary **is** changing all the time.   **b.** New words **are** added frequently.

Which sentence has a singular subject? ___a.___ Underline the boldfaced verb in that sentence.

Which sentence has a plural subject? ___b.___ Circle the boldfaced verb in that sentence.

> **Am, is, was, are,** and **were** are forms of the verb **be**. Use *am* after the pronoun *I*. Use *is* or *was* after a singular subject or after the pronoun *he*, *she*, or *it*. Use *are* or *were* after a plural subject or after the pronoun *we*, *you*, or *they*.

Practice

Underline the subject of each sentence. Then circle the correct form of *be* to complete the verb.

1. I (**am**/are) wondering where some of the words we use originated.

2. How (was/**were**) names picked for places?

3. (**Are**/Is) any names in your state Native American words?

4. The name of my favorite food (**was**/were) borrowed from the Spanish language.

5. Tacos (**are**/is) a delicious combination of meat and vegetables.

6. We add words as we need them. (Was/**Were**) the Pilgrims using the word *television*?

7. Can you think of any words that we (is/**are**) using today that we didn't need years ago?

8. The word *splashdown* (**was**/were) unknown one hundred years ago.

9. Some modern words (was/**were**) created from ancient sources.

10. *Astro* (**is**/are) from the Greek word *astron*, meaning "star," and *naut* (**is**/are) from the Greek word *nautes*, meaning "sailor."

11. Do you think *astronaut* (are/**is**) a good name for the people who fly our spaceships?

Strategies for Writers—**Conventions & Skills Practice   Unit 4**

Apply

Rewrite each sentence. Add a form of the word *be* to complete each sentence correctly.

12. There _____ groups of words that are special to certain areas. _____

    There are groups of words that are special to certain areas.

13. Which school subject _____ most likely to need the words *add* and *subtract*?

    Which school subject is most likely to need the words *add* and *subtract*?

14. For which sport _____ phrases like *home run* and *base hit* created? _____

    For which sport were phrases like *home run* and *base hit* created?

15. Sometimes we blend two words together to make a new word. What words _____ put together to make *motel*?

    Sometimes we blend two words together to make a new word. Which words were put together to make *motel*?

16. The words that _____ blended are *motor* and *hotel*. _____

    The words that were/are blended are *motor* and *hotel*.

17. One word _____ created by blending *smoke* and *fog*. _____

    One word was created by blending *smoke* and *fog*.

18. Some words have nearly the same meaning. They _____ called synonyms.

    Some words have nearly the same meaning. They are called synonyms.

19. An antonym _____ a word with the opposite meaning of another word. _____

    An antonym is a word with the opposite meaning of another word.

20. The sandwich some people call a poor boy _____ called a submarine by others.

    The sandwich some people call a poor boy is called a submarine by others.

Verb Tense

Learn

In 1812, Robert Browning **was born** in a suburb of London, England. At that time, England and the United States **were fighting** the War of 1812. His father's library **is** the source of Browning's education.

Circle the boldfaced verb or verb phrase that does not give a correct sense of time.

> All words in a sentence must work together to give an accurate sense of time. Make sure each **verb** is in the **proper tense** for the time period being discussed.

Practice

Circle the verb or verb phrase that gives the correct sense of time.

1. Robert Browning (was/had been) one of the greatest Victorian poets.

2. Browning's optimism (is reflected/will be reflected) in his famous line, "All's right with the world!"

3. Browning's first poem, a narrative titled "Pauline," (is published/was published) in 1833.

4. Gradually, Browning (develops/developed) a style called the dramatic monologue, a poem told by an imaginary person.

5. In 1845, Robert Browning (meets/met) the poet Elizabeth Barrett.

6. He (is writing/had been writing) to her because he greatly admired her poems.

7. Elizabeth's father (did not approve/will not approve) of the marriage between Robert and Elizabeth.

8. Because of her father's disapproval, the couple (is deciding/decided) to be married secretly.

9. After their marriage in 1846, Elizabeth and Robert (had lived/lived) in Italy.

10. Elizabeth Barrett Browning's best-known work for modern readers (is/will be) *Sonnets from the Portuguese,* a collection of poems about her romance with Robert Browning.

Rewrite the following sentences to show that the events took place in the past.

11. Robert Browning is writing many narrative poems and plays. _____

   Robert Browning (wrote/was writing) many narrative poems and plays.
   _____

12. Then he develops his best-known style, the dramatic monologue. _____

   Then he developed his best-known style, the dramatic monologue.
   _____

13. Browning likes to write about people who live during the Renaissance, a time when the arts flourished.

   Browning liked to write about people who lived during the Renaissance, a time when
   _____

   the arts flourished.
   _____

14. Browning dislikes being passive and is wanting to experience everything he could.

   Browning disliked being passive and wanted to experience everything he could.
   _____

   _____

15. Because he prefers action, he will use rapid movement in his poems. _____

   Because he preferred action, he used rapid movement in his poems.
   _____

16. Browning shows a sense of realism by writing about evil characters as well as good characters.

   Browning showed a sense of realism by writing about evil characters as well as good characters.
   _____

   _____

17. In his poem "Pied Piper of Hamelin," Browning writes about a mythical character who lured pests and children away from a town.

   In his poem "Pied Piper of Hamelin," Browning wrote about a mythical character who lured pests
   _____

   and children away from a town.
   _____

18. Now considered a great poet, Browning is not recognized as such until he is almost 60 years old.

   Now considered a great poet, Browning was not recognized as such until he was almost
   _____

   60 years old.
   _____

Verbs and Compound Subjects

Learn

a. (Some words and phrases) have more than one meaning.

b. Often (a word or a phrase) has a denotation and a connotation.

Circle the compound subject in each sentence. Underline the verb in each sentence.

Which sentence, **a.** or **b.**, has a verb that goes with a singular subject? ___**b.**___

> A **compound subject** and its **verb** must agree. If a compound subject includes the conjunction *and*, it is plural and needs a plural verb. If a compound subject includes *or* or *nor*, the verb must agree with the last item in the subject.

Practice

Find the compound subject in each sentence. Circle the conjunction. Underline the correct verb.

1. Some words (and) phrases with similar definitions (suggest/suggests) very different meanings.

2. The dictionary definition (or) literal definition of a word (are/is) that word's denotative meaning.

3. Words (and) phrases also (possess/possesses) an emotional or a connotative meaning.

4. *Childlike* (and) *childish* (have/has) the same denotative, or literal, meanings; both mean "having the characteristics of a child."

5. Games (and) puzzles (furnishes/furnish) opportunities for childlike activities.

6. However, selfishness (or) temper tantrums (shows/show) childish behavior.

7. Poets (and) novelists (chooses/choose) certain words based on the words' connotations.

8. A scientific paper (or) a set of directions (use/uses) exact words with clear meanings.

9. Symbols (and) formulas (gives/give) the precise information that scientists need.

10. A camper (and) a firefighter (sense/senses) different connotative, or emotional, meanings for *flames*.

11. *House* (and) *home* (refer/refers) to the same object, but *home* has a warmer feeling.

12. An expert canoeist (and) a non-swimmer probably (define/defines) *rapids* differently.

Rewrite these sentences to correct the errors.

13. Describing and telling is two ways a writer can get a point across. _____

Describing and telling are two ways a writer can get a point across.

14. An active image or a dull picture are often the result of the choice. _____

An active image or a dull picture is often the result of the choice.

15. Robert Louis Stevenson and Elizabeth Coatsworth provides interesting word choices for a train.

Robert Louis Stevenson and Elizabeth Coatsworth provide interesting word choices for a train.

16. *Snuffs* and *snorts* is words from Coatsworth's poem "The Ways of Trains." _____

Snuffs *and* *snorts* *are words from Coatsworth's poem "The Ways of Trains."*

17. Either *blow* or *toot* are an equally good word to tell about a train's whistle. _____

Either *blow* *or* *toot* *is an equally good word to tell about a train's whistle.*

18. Poets and other writers spends lots of time choosing exactly the right word. _____

Poets and other writers spend lots of time choosing exactly the right word.

19. *Cheap* and *thrifty* has similar denotations but very different connotations.

Cheap *and* *thrifty* *have similar denotations but very different connotations.*

20. A villain or some other evil character are more likely to be called cheap.

A villain or some other evil character is more likely to be called cheap.

Comparing with Adjectives and Adverbs

Learn

When they were young, Elizabeth Barrett Browning was **more famous** than her husband, Robert Browning. Her poems were among the (**most popular**) poems of that era.

Underline the boldfaced adjective that compares two people. Circle the boldfaced adjective that compares three or more things.

> The **comparative form** of an **adjective** or an **adverb** compares two people, places, things, or actions. Add *-er* to short adjectives or adverbs to create the comparative form. Use the word *more* before long adjectives and adverbs to create the comparative form (*more careful*).
>
> The **superlative form** compares three or more people, places, things, or actions. Add *-est* to create the superlative form. Use the word *most* before long adjectives and adverbs to create the superlative form (*most carefully*). Use the words *better* and *less* to compare two things. Use *best* and *least* to compare three or more things.

Practice

Circle the correct form of the adjective or adverb in parentheses.

1. At home, Elizabeth Barrett received the (better/**best**) education available in languages and literature.

2. It was said that Elizabeth's father was the (harsher/**harshest**) parent a child could have.

3. In 1821, Elizabeth injured her spine in a fall, but an even (**more shocking**/most shocking) event occurred when her brother drowned in 1838.

4. After these tragedies, Elizabeth spent (**less**/least) time around friends and family and more time in her room.

5. She felt it was (**better**/best) to write letters and poems than to face the world.

6. Perhaps the (greater/**greatest**) admirer of Elizabeth's poems was Robert Browning.

7. When Elizabeth and Robert finally met, they became (**more strongly**/most strongly) attached to each other.

8. In time, Robert's poems were considered (**greater**/greatest) than Elizabeth's.

Rewrite each sentence, adding the correct form of the adjective or adverb in parentheses.

9. The firm opinion of Elizabeth's father became even _____ when it came to giving permission for his sons and daughters to marry. (strong)

The firm opinion of Elizabeth's father became even stronger when it came to giving permission for his

sons and daughters to marry.

10. Elizabeth and Robert became engaged over the _____ objections her father ever expressed. (violent)

Elizabeth and Robert became engaged over the most violent objections her father ever expressed.

11. Their romance became even _____ when they married secretly and left England for Italy. (dramatic)

Their romance became even more dramatic when they married secretly and left England for Italy.

12. In Italy, Elizabeth grew _____ than she had been in England. (healthy) _____

In Italy, Elizabeth grew healthier than she had been in England.

13. The _____ event of all, though, was the birth of their son. (exciting) _____

The most exciting event of all, though, was the birth of their son.

14. Elizabeth continued to write, and no female poet of the time was held in _____ esteem. (high)

Elizabeth continued to write, and no female poet of the time was held in higher esteem.

15. Some of her poetry addressed perhaps the _____ social issue of the time, slavery. (important)

Some of her poetry addressed perhaps the most important social issue of the time, slavery.

16. Of all her works, her verse novel Aurora Leigh is probably her _____ accomplishment. (great)

Of all her works, her verse novel Aurora Leigh is probably her greatest accomplishment.

Auxiliary Verbs

Learn

Rachel Carson saw that pesticides (could) **be** a threat to human food supplies. She knew that she (must) **write** about this danger.

Underline the main verb in boldface in each sentence. Circle the auxiliary verb in boldface that works with each main verb.

> An **auxiliary verb,** or **helping verb,** works with a main verb. Auxiliary verbs have different purposes. Some auxiliary verbs, such as *could, should, might,* and *may,* show how likely it is that something will happen. Some auxiliary verbs, such as *did, is, will,* and *would,* indicate the tense of the main verb.

Practice

Circle the correct auxiliary verb.

1. Sometimes an author writes a book that (can/is) arouse public opinion.

2. Rachel Carson (should be/is) credited for such a book.

3. In *Silent Spring,* she pointed out how pesticides (could/should) poison the food supplies of animals.

4. She also suggested that pesticides (might/was) contaminate human food supplies sooner or later.

5. Her arguments (is/were) meant to inform people about the dangers of pesticides.

6. Another writer whose work (will/would) arouse public opinion was Thomas Paine.

7. Paine's pamphlet *Common Sense* (may/would) inspire the American colonists to seek independence from England.

8. A Harriet Beecher Stowe novel (was/may) have helped start the Civil War.

9. Her famous book, *Uncle Tom's Cabin,* (would/should) intensify feelings about the issue of slavery.

Complete each sentence with the correct auxiliary verb. Some sentences have more than one correct answer.

10. Like Carson and Paine, Stowe _____ **was** _____ both praised and criticized intensely for the ideas she advanced.

11. Carson _____ **will/may/might** _____ be remembered most for *Silent Spring,* but she also wrote other well-received books, including *The Sea Around Us.*

12. In her writings, she stressed how the well-being of one living thing _____ **can/may/will** _____ affect other living things.

13. Stowe also wrote other books, including ones that _____ **would** _____ show the positive and negative sides of Puritanism.

14. Paine's later pamphlets _____ **would/did** _____ encourage the Continental Army during the darkest days of the Revolutionary War.

15. Thomas Paine _____ **would** _____ continue to write all his life, and his ideas

    _____ **would** _____ continue to evoke strong responses.

16. He defended the French Revolution, and as a result he _____ **was** _____ tried for treason by the English government.

17. Upton Sinclair is another writer who _____ **could/did** _____ stir up calls for reform.

18. He _____ **was** _____ called a muckraker because he raked up various social and political evils.

19. His most famous book, *The Jungle,* _____ **would** _____ lead to the passage of the nation's first pure food laws.

20. Coal mining conditions _____ **were** _____ attacked in Sinclair's book *King Coal.*

21. Some of Sinclair's books _____ **were/had been** _____ crafted more carefully than others, perhaps because he was more interested in the issues than in the art of writing.

Writing Sentences Correctly

Learn

a. Wow, look at how high they leaped!

b. How did they ever learn to do that?

c. I understand it takes years of practice.

d. Watch how they are spinning around.

Which sentence asks a question? ___b.___ Circle its end mark.

Which sentence gives a command? ___d.___ Circle its end mark.

Which sentence shows excitement? ___a.___ Circle its end mark.

Which sentence makes a statement? ___c.___ Circle its end mark.

> Begin every **sentence** with a **capital letter**. A **declarative** sentence makes a statement and ends with a **period**. An **interrogative** sentence asks a question and ends with a **question mark**. An **imperative** sentence gives a command and ends with a **period** or an **exclamation point**. An **exclamatory** sentence shows excitement and ends with an **exclamation point**.

Practice

Each sentence is either declarative (DE), interrogative (INT), imperative (IMP), or exclamatory (EX). Label each sentence **DE, INT, IMP,** or **EX**.

1. Ballet is a special kind of dancing that is performed for theater audiences.   ___DE___

2. Is it very different from other kinds of dancing?   ___INT___

3. It sure is!   ___EX___

4. Imagine dancing on the tips of your toes!   ___IMP/EX___

5. Can you imagine spinning like a top without losing your balance?   ___INT___

6. Ballet dancers make difficult yet graceful movements look easy and natural.   ___DE___

7. Gee, how hard they must work!   ___EX___

8. Tell me more about their training.   ___IMP___

Rewrite each sentence. Add capital letters and end marks of punctuation.

9. how long has ballet been around _____

How long has ballet been around?

10. historians believe the first ballet was performed in 1581 _____

Historians believe the first ballet was performed in 1581.

11. it lasted 5 1/2 hours It lasted 5 1/2 hours. _____

12. tell me more about that long performance _____

Tell me more about that long performance.

13. it was performed in honor of a royal wedding _____

It was performed in honor of a royal wedding.

14. did the performers wear tutus and tights in the 1580s _____

Did the performers wear tutus and tights in the 1580s?

15. no, they wore fancy, heavy costumes that came to the floor _____

No, they wore fancy, heavy costumes that came to the floor.

16. ugh, I would not like that Ugh, I would not like that! _____

17. how did they dance in those costumes _____

How did they dance in those costumes?

18. dances were simpler, so the costumes did not bother them _____

Dances were simpler, so the costumes did not bother them.

19. explain when and how costumes got simpler _____

Explain when and how costumes got simpler.

20. people who designed ballets began to produce story lines that were very romantic

People who designed ballets began to produce story lines that were very romantic.

_____

Proper Nouns and Proper Adjectives

Learn

There have been many famous ballet dancers from (Russia). (St. Petersburg) was home to (Vaslav Nijinsky) and (Anna Pavlova), two of the most famous ballet dancers of all time.

Circle the words that name specific people, places, or things.

> A common noun names a person, place, thing, or idea. A **proper noun** names a specific person, place, thing, or idea. The important words in proper nouns are **capitalized**. **Proper adjectives** are descriptive words formed from proper nouns. They must be capitalized. A **title of respect,** such as *Mr.* or *Judge,* is used before a person's name. *I* is also capitalized.

Practice

Circle lowercase letters that should be capital letters. Draw a line through capital letters that should be lowercase. (**1.–5.**)

1. nijinsky thrilled audiences with his magnificent leaps, and anna Pavlova was World Famous for her Grace. Pavlova and Nijinsky worked with a company named the Ballets russes. A man Named michel Fokine was a choreographer with the Ballets russes. He created wonderful works, such as *Prince Igor* and *The firebird*.

2. Three famous russian dancers, Rudolf nureyev, natalia Makarova, and Mikhail baryshnikov, defected to the West. Nureyev was in paris when he left the kirov Ballet. In 1962, he formed a Partnership with the famous english ballerina dame margot fonteyn.

3. Dame margot Fonteyn is perhaps the greatest british ballerina of all Time. Many ballets were created especially for her by sir Frederick ashton. The ballet ondine was the vehicle for some of her greatest performances.

4. By the mid-1900s, no one Country was the leader in ballet. United states' stars included the ballerinas melissa Hayden and nora Kaye. One of the leading male Dancers was erik Bruhn of denmark.

5. Today, many dancers tour throughout the World. Choreographers stage their works in Nations other than their own. Institutions such as the american Dance festival offer scholarships to foreign students. The movements and the Music of a ballet speak a Language that can be understood in any country.

Rewrite these sentences to correct the errors.

6. The Atlanta civic Ballet invited other nonprofessional ballet Companies to a ballet festival in 1956.

   The Atlanta Civic Ballet invited other nonprofessional ballet companies to a ballet festival in 1956.

7. The festival was a Big success and led to the formation of the Southeastern regional Ballet festival Association.

   The festival was a big success and led to the formation of the Southeastern Regional Ballet Festival

   Association.

8. By 1990, there were five regional ballet Associations in the united states.

   By 1990, there were five regional ballet associations in the United States.

9. Each regional association holds an Annual festival.

   Each regional association holds an annual festival.

10. The festivals are of such high Quality that they have raised the standard of ballet throughout the Country.

    The festivals are of such high quality that they have raised the standard of ballet throughout

    the country.

11. Many european countries provide government support of the arts, including ballet.

    Many European countries provide government support of the arts, including ballet.

12. The Governments of new Zealand, australia, and Canada also provide government support.

    The governments of New Zealand, Australia, and Canada also provide government support.

Initials and Abbreviations

Learn

<u>Mr.</u> Ogden <u>P.</u> Krafts, an expert on motion pictures, visited our class last week. I went to his office to invite him, and he made a note about the appointment. The note said, "(Tues.), (Mar.) 6, [Mrs.] Willis, Parker School."

Draw a square around a short way to write *Mistress*. Underline a short way to write *Mister*. Circle short ways to write *Tuesday* and *March*. Underline a letter that stands for a name.

> An **abbreviation** is a shortened form of a word. **Titles of respect** are usually abbreviated. So are words in addresses such as *Street* (*St.*), *Avenue* (*Ave.*), and *Boulevard* (*Blvd.*). **Days,** some **months,** and parts of **business names** (*Co.* for *Company*) are often abbreviated in informal notes. Abbreviations usually begin with a capital letter and end with a period. An **initial** can replace a person's or a place's name. It is written as a capital letter followed by a period.

Practice

Circle lowercase letters that should be capital letters. Draw a line through capital letters that should be lowercase letters. Add periods where they are needed. (**1.–20.**)

Mr. Ogden P. Krafts spoke briefly about the beginning of motion pictures in the u.s. He said that Thomas a. Edison gave the first public exhibition of projected moving pictures on April 23, 1896. He said that Edwin s. Porter's 1903 film, *The Great Train Robbery*, was the first film to tell a story. Storytelling films started the trend that led to nickelodeons, the earliest motion Picture theaters.

Mrs. Willis, our teacher, asked about some of the early Stars. mr. Krafts named Douglas Fairbanks, Mary Pickford, William s. hart, a cowboy star, and the comedian Charlie Chaplin.

Mr. Krafts reminded us that the very first films were silent. The first important Talking movie, or "talkie," as they were first called, was *The Jazz Singer*, with Al jolson.

Mr. Krafts pointed out to us that a two-week moviemaking exhibit was coming to the science museum on aug. 18. He reminded us that the museum is on the corner of State St. and Olive blvd. He said that his company, Technics co., will be Sponsoring the event. He will serve as a coordinator of events.

Rewrite this announcement. Use abbreviations and initials where you can. (**21.–29.**)

The Clarksburg Science Museum and Technics Company
proudly announce the exhibition
"The Art and Science of Movies: Moviemaking Through the Years"
Clarksburg Science Museum
State Street and Olive Boulevard
Tuesday, August 18—Monday, September 1
Coordinator of Events: Mister Ogden Percival Krafts

The Clarksburg Science Museum and Technics Co.
_____

proudly announce the exhibition
_____

"The Art and Science of Movies: Moviemaking Through the Years"
_____

Clarksburg Science Museum
_____

State St. and Olive Blvd.
_____

Tues., Aug. 18—Mon., Sept. 1
_____

Coordinator of Events: Mr. O. P. Krafts
_____

_____

_____

_____

30. Write a note to yourself to attend the opening preview on Monday, August 17. You are to call Mistress Willis to find out what time the preview begins. **Answers will vary.**
Possible answers appear below.

Call Mrs. Willis—
_____

Movies exhibition
_____

What time preview Mon., Aug. 17?
_____

_____

_____

Titles

Learn

Mrs. Willis pointed out that many movies are based on books or plays. For example, the movie (Hamlet) is based on William Shakespeare's play. Maria asked if a movie had been made based on the poem "The Song of Hiawatha."

Circle the movie title. Draw a box around the poem title. How are they written differently?

The movie title is underlined. The title of the poem has quotation marks.

_____

> Underline **book titles** and **movie titles**. Use **quotation marks** around the titles of **songs, stories,** and **poems**. **Capitalize** the first word and last word in titles. Capitalize all other words except articles, prepositions, and conjunctions. Remember to capitalize short verbs, such as *is* and *are*.

Practice

Circle each lowercase letter that should be a capital letter. Underline and add quotation marks where you need to.

1. One of my favorite songs is "Over the rainbow." It is from the movie The wizard of oz.

2. We discussed whether Poe's poem "the raven" would make a good movie.

3. We agreed that Poe's short story "the Purloined letter" could be adapted for the screen.

4. Mrs. Willis asked if we knew of any books that had been made into movies. Carlos mentioned Where the red fern Grows.

5. I named sense and sensibility. Maria named dr. Jekyll and mr. hyde.

6. Alisha pointed out that the animated movie the lion king had been made into a stage play.

7. Mrs. Willis suddenly remembered a poem, "gunga din," that had been made into a movie.

8. Jake said that movies sometimes include a good song. One song he likes is "I'll Get by," from the movie A guy named joe.

Follow the directions to write one or two sentences. Include the title of a book, movie, song, story, or poem in your sentences. **Answers will vary. The required marks are shown below.**

9. Which movie currently playing do you most want to see? Why?

[Underline the movie title.]

_____

_____

10. Describe the worst movie you have ever seen.

[Underline the title.]

_____

_____

11. Recommend a poem to a friend.

[Quotation marks around the title of the poem.]

_____

_____

12. Tell something about a story you read in class.

[Quotation marks around the title of the story.]

_____

_____

13. What is your favorite song, and why do you like it?

[Quotation marks around the title of the song.]

_____

_____

14. Tell something about an exciting book you have read.

[Underline the book title.]

_____

_____

15. Tell why a certain story or book would make a good movie.

[Quotation marks around the title of a story; underline a book title and the movie title.]

_____

_____

16. Tell why you don't like a particular song or poem.

[Quotation marks around the title of the song or poem.]

_____

_____

Apostrophes

Learn

Some of Georgia **O'Keeffe's** most famous paintings include flowers or animal skulls or both.
Most people **wouldn't** think of animal bones as art subjects.

Which boldfaced word shows possession or ownership?   O'Keeffe's

Which boldfaced word is a combination of two words?   wouldn't

> To form the **possessive** of a singular noun, add an apostrophe and -s
> (*artist's work*). For plural nouns that end in s, add an apostrophe (*critics'*
> *choice*). For plural nouns that do not end in s, add an apostrophe and -s
> (*women's show*). **Apostrophes** are also used in **contractions,** two words
> that have been shortened and combined.

Practice

Circle the correct word in parentheses. If the answer is a possessive, write **possessive**. If the
answer is a contraction, write the two words that made the contraction.

1. O'Keeffe's mother (couldn't/could'nt) believe that Georgia
   could recall and describe so many things from her infancy.   could not

2. Georgia could describe scenes from years past so completely
   that her (mother's/mothers') doubts were removed.   possessive

3. When she was in school, she (did'nt/didn't) always agree
   with the teachers.   did not

4. One of (O'Keeffe's/O'Keeffes) personality traits from the time
   she was young was that she always had her own ideas.   possessive

5. She (wasn't/was'nt) happy painting strictly according to her
   various (teachers'/teacher's) ideas.   was not

   possessive

6. She realized that she (could'nt/couldn't) live where she
   wanted to or go where she wanted to, but she could paint
   as she wanted to.   could not

Apply

Rewrite these sentences. Replace the boldfaced words with possessives or contractions.

7. O'Keeffe married and moved to the **30th floor of the Shelton Hotel**. _____

   O'Keeffe married and moved to the Shelton Hotel's 30th floor.
   _____

8. There O'Keeffe painted pictures in styles she **had not** used before. _____

   There O'Keeffe painted pictures in styles she hadn't used before.
   _____

9. These paintings captured the **excitement of the city**. _____

   These paintings captured the city's excitement.
   _____

10. The **reactions of people** were positive. _____

    The people's reactions were positive.
    _____

11. Then O'Keeffe went to Taos, where she fell in love with **the beauty of New Mexico**.

    Then O'Keeffe went to Taos, where she fell in love with New Mexico's beauty.
    _____

    _____

12. After her husband died, O'Keeffe **did not** return to the East. _____

    After her husband died, O'Keeffe didn't return to the East.
    _____

13. She started painting **the skulls of animals** because she felt she **could not** do justice to the desert landscape.

    She started painting animals' skulls because she felt she couldn't do justice to the desert landscape.
    _____

    _____

14. Before O'Keeffe, some critics considered **the art of women** inferior to **the art of men**.

    Before O'Keeffe, some critics considered women's art inferior to men's art.
    _____

    _____

15. Whatever she painted, the main characteristic of **the work of O'Keeffe** is that she was always herself.

    Whatever she painted, the main characteristic of O'Keeffe's work is that she was always herself.
    _____

    _____

Commas in a Series

Learn

a. The City Symphony played works by Mozart, Tchaikovsky, and Dvořák.

b. Mozart, one of the most productive of composers, wrote two of the works we heard.

Circle the commas in each sentence.
In which sentence do the commas separate three items in a series? _____a._____

> A **series** is a list of three or more words or phrases. **Commas** are used to separate items in a series. Each item in a series might consist of one word or a longer phrase. The last comma in a series goes before the conjunction (*and, or*). A comma is not needed to separate two items.

Practice

Add commas where they are needed in the sentences. Cross out commas that should not be there.

1. The word *symphony* can mean a certain style of musical composition, a group of musical instruments, or the musicians who play these compositions.

2. In the seventeenth century, *symphony* meant a musical composition for instruments, an instrumental introduction, or a piece between parts of an opera.

3. The symphonic form was developed from the overtures, and introductory pieces to Italian operas.

4. The usual four parts of a classical symphony are a fast movement, a slow movement, a dance movement, and another fast movement.

5. These parts are called the Allegro, the Andante, the Scherzo, and the Allegro.

6. The opening movement is usually made up of the exposition, the development, and the recapitulation.

7. The composers like to use a specific form, develop themes, and write variations on those themes.

8. The Classical Period of music followed the Baroque Period and is considered to be from 1750 to 1820.

Rewrite each group of sentences as a single sentence. Use commas and the conjunction **and** or **or** to join items in a series. Answers may vary. Possible responses appear below.

9. Do you think Haydn is the best composer of symphonies?
Do you think Mozart is the best composer of symphonies?
Do you think Beethoven is the best composer of symphonies?

Do you think Haydn, Mozart, or Beethoven is the best composer of symphonies?

_____

_____

10. Joseph Haydn wrote more than 80 works for strings.
Joseph Haydn wrote more than 100 works for full symphonies.
Joseph Haydn wrote other works for voices.

Joseph Haydn wrote more than 80 works for strings, more than 100 works for full symphonies, and

other works for voices.

_____

11. Wolfgang Amadeus Mozart wrote 42 symphonies.
Wolfgang Amadeus Mozart wrote 22 operas.
Wolfgang Amadeus Mozart wrote 27 piano concertos.

Wolfgang Amadeus Mozart wrote 42 symphonies, 22 operas, and 27 piano concertos.

_____

_____

12. Ludwig van Beethoven's symphonies are still performed today.
Beethoven's operas are still performed today.
His piano sonatas are still performed today.

Ludwig van Beethoven's symphonies, operas, and piano sonatas are still performed today.

_____

_____

More Uses of Commas

Learn

"Luis, are you going to the piano concert on Saturday?" Donella asked.
"Yes, Dad is taking my sister and me, and we're going to sit in the first row!"

Who is being spoken to in the first sentence? _____Luis_____

What punctuation mark comes after the name? _____comma_____

What word introduces the second sentence? _____Yes_____

What punctuation mark follows it? _____comma_____

What conjunction joins the two independent clauses in the second sentence? _____and_____

What punctuation mark comes before it? _____comma_____

> **Commas** tell a reader where to pause. A comma is used to separate an **introductory word** from the rest of a sentence. It is used with a conjunction to join the **independent clauses** in a **compound sentence** and to separate a **noun of direct address** from the rest of a sentence. A noun of direct address names a person who is being spoken to.

Practice

Add the missing comma to each sentence. Then decide why the comma is needed. Write **I** for introductory word, **C** for compound sentence, or **D** for direct address.

1. The concert featured music by Beethoven, but there was one piece by Mozart. ___C___

2. Wow, that was an exciting concert! ___I___

3. "Cassie, help me do some research about Beethoven's life," Gordon said. ___D___

4. "Sure, I'll be glad to go with you to the library," Cassie agreed. ___I___

5. Beethoven was born in Germany in 1770, and he died in 1827. ___C___

6. He gradually lost his ability to hear, but he composed music until his death. ___C___

7. "He wrote 38 sonatas for the piano, and three of them were composed when he was 10 years old!" exclaimed Cassie. ___C___

8. "Cassie, let's go practice!" shouted Gordon. ___D___

Strategies for Writers—Conventions & Skills Practice   Unit 5

Rewrite the sentences by adding the words in parentheses. You will turn all sentence pairs into one sentence.

9. Ludwig van Beethoven's music is divided into three periods. (and) He wrote many musical pieces in each period.

   Ludwig van Beethoven's music is divided into three periods, and he wrote many musical pieces

   in each period.

10. Beethoven's second period, from about 1800 to 1815, was his most productive. (but) Three of his five piano concertos were written earlier.

    Beethoven's second period, from about 1800 to 1815, was his most productive, but three of his

    five piano concertos were written earlier.

11. (My goodness) Beethoven must have worked on his compositions many years before he published them!

    My goodness, Beethoven must have worked on his compositions many years before he

    published them!

12. (Yes) He was a very careful composer. _____

    Yes, he was a very careful composer.

13. Beethoven's work is very popular today. (but) His new ideas were hard for people to understand during his lifetime.

    Beethoven's work is very popular today, but his new ideas were hard for people to understand

    during his lifetime.

14. Many symphonies are known by their number. (but) Some have descriptive names.

    Many symphonies are known by their number, but some have descriptive names.

15. Let's find out about modern symphonies. (Gordon) _____

    Gordon, let's find out about modern symphonies.

16. (Oh) I know just where to look. _____

    Oh, I know just where to look.

Using Colons and Semicolons

Learn

a. In the 1800s, painters became dissatisfied with the neoclassic and romantic styles; these styles seemed stale and artificial to them.

b. The new, realistic style they developed consisted of the following: an accurate depiction of life, authentic detail, and a deliberate look at life's problems.

Which sentence, **a.** or **b.**, is a compound sentence? __a.__ What punctuation mark is used to join the two independent clauses in this compound sentence? __;__ Which sentence includes a list of items? __b.__ What punctuation mark introduces this list? __:__

> A **semicolon** can be used instead of a comma and conjunction to join the independent clauses in a **compound sentence**. A **colon** is used before lists in sentences, especially after words such as *the following* or *as follows*.

Practice

Add the missing semicolons and colons to these sentences.

1. Early settlers in North America had little leisure time; they were too busy taming the wilderness.

2. American artists had little use for the classical, European style; a strong tradition of realism quickly developed among American painters.

3. Beginning in the 1800s, America produced a number of realistic painters such as the following: William Harnett, John Peto, Thomas Eakins, and Robert Henri.

4. One group of painters particularly liked the scenery along the Hudson River; they became known as the Hudson River School.

5. Winslow Homer was drawn to the sea; he painted many scenes of the Atlantic Ocean.

6. Many art movements appeared during the 1900s among them were the following: fauvism, cubism, and abstract expressionism.

7. In 1908, an American group exhibited paintings; most were realistic scenes of ordinary people.

8. The Great Depression of the 1930s produced a number of American realists such as the following: Grant Wood, Thomas Hart Benton, John Steuart Curry, and William Gropper.

Apply

Copy each independent clause below. Then add another independent clause to form a compound sentence or add a list. Use semicolons and colons correctly in your sentence.

9. To paint a picture you need the following: [list]

_____

_____

10. The realistic style in art began in the 1800s; [independent clause]

_____

_____

11. Realistic painters like to paint the following: [list]

_____

_____

12. Some modern art can bewilder a viewer; [independent clause]

_____

_____

13. A visit to an art museum should not be hurried; [independent clause]

_____

_____

14. An artist's palette should include the following colors: [list]

_____

_____

15. Museums and art galleries can be found in nearly every American town or city;

[independent clause]

_____

16. Today, American art is the equal of any in the world; [independent clause]

_____

Direct and Indirect Quotations

Learn

a. Jeannine asked, "Have you read the comic page today?"

b. LeRoy answered that he had not read it yet.

Which sentence, **a.** or **b.,** shows a speaker's exact words? ___a.___
Circle the marks that begin and end these words.
Underline the first letter of the quotation.

> A **direct quotation** is a speaker's exact words. Use **quotation marks** at the beginning and end of a direct quotation. Begin a direct quotation with a capital letter. Use a comma or end punctuation to separate the speaker's exact words from the rest of the sentence. An **indirect quotation** is a retelling of a speaker's words. Do not use quotation marks when the word *that* or *whether* comes before a speaker's words.

Practice

Write **I** after each indirect quotation and **D** after each direct quotation. Then add quotation marks, commas, and end marks to direct quotations. Draw three lines (≡) under lowercase letters that should be capitalized.

1. Our art teacher explained that cartooning is one style of art that tells a story. ___I___

2. She explained that a cartoon was once an artist's practice drawing. ___I___

3. Joshua asked, "how many kinds of cartoons are there?" ___D___

4. Ms. Ortiz replied, "There are editorial cartoons, single panel cartoons, illustrative cartoons, and advertising cartoons." ___D___

5. Joshua wanted to know whether the illustrations in library books could be considered cartoons. ___I___

6. Ms. Ortiz replied that many library books do have cartoon illustrations. ___I___

7. She said, "let's look at some examples of books you read when you were younger." ___D___

8. Maria said that *In the Night Kitchen* by Maurice Sendak is a good example. ___I___

9. "How about the books of Dr. Seuss?" asked Halle. ___D___

10. "I liked *Oh, the Places You'll Go!* by Dr. Seuss," said Maria. ___D___

Strategies for Writers—Conventions & Skills Practice   Unit 5

Rewrite each indirect quotation as a direct quotation. Rewrite each direct quotation as an indirect quotation. (There may be more than one right way to do this.) Use punctuation marks correctly.

11. Mom said that her favorite cartoonist is Cathy Guisewite. _____

    Mom said, "Cathy Guisewite is my favorite cartoonist."

12. "Her character Cathy is a lot like I used to be," she said. _____

    She said that the character Cathy is a lot like she used to be.

13. I said that I have read that Guisewite uses her own mother and father for ideas.

    "I've read that Guisewite used her own mother and father for ideas," I said.

14. "I guess that explains why they seem so real," Mom said. _____

    Mom said that she guessed that's why they seem so real.

15. Sarah said that her mother's favorite cartoonist is Lynn Johnston. _____

    Sarah said, "My mother's favorite cartoonist is Lynn Johnston."

16. Sarah said, "Mother believes the family in Johnston's strip is like our family sometimes."

    She said that her mother thinks the family in Johnston's strip is like their family.

17. We asked Ms. Ortiz whether cartoon artists draw with pencils and crayons or with brushes.

    We asked, "Ms. Ortiz, do cartoon artists draw with pencils and crayons or with brushes?"

18. "Some do both, but more and more are using computer graphics," she explained.

    She explained that some do both, but more and more are using computer graphics.

19. Ms. Ortiz suggested we try imitating a favorite cartoonist's style. _____

    She suggested, "Why don't you try imitating your favorite cartoonist's style?"

20. "I'll look at cartoons in a completely different way now," said Sarah. _____

    Sarah said that now she'll look at cartoons in a completely different way.

Friendly Letters and Business Letters

French Creek Arts Camp
French Creek, Oklahoma 74077-6821
June 16, 2003

(Dear Martha,)

French Creek is beautiful. Yesterday we did watercolors by the creek. Tomorrow we are going to use colored chalk to draw the trees. I am learning a lot, but I am also having a lot of fun.

Your friend,

Lee

There are five different parts of this letter. Two have already been circled. Circle the other three.

A **friendly letter** has five parts. The **heading** gives your address and the date. The **greeting** includes the name of the person to whom you are writing. It begins with a capital letter and ends with a comma. The **body** gives your message. The **closing** is a friendly way to say good-bye. It ends with a comma. The **signature** is your name. A friendly letter is written to someone you know and may include informal language.

A **business letter** is a formal letter written to an employer or a business. It has the same parts as a friendly letter, but it also includes the complete address of the person to whom you are writing. In a business letter, write a colon after the greeting.

Practice

Label the five parts of the friendly letter below. Write the name of each part on the line next to it.

1. ___**heading**___   1841 West Adams Street
Kirkwood, Missouri 63126-2430
July 3, 2003

Dear Lee,   2. ___**greeting**___

   I am so glad that you are enjoying the arts camp. Kirk and I are working very hard on decorating an arts club float for the Fourth of July Parade. We could use some of those skills you are learning! 3. ___**body**___

4. ___**closing**___   Your friend,

5. ___**signature**___   Martha

Strategies for Writers—Conventions & Skills Practice

Rewrite this business letter correctly on the lines below. Remember that the sender's address and the date go on the right. The business address goes on the left. (**6.–12.**)

Riverside Art Books 314 Donnybrook Drive St. Louis, MO 63128-2640 Dear Sir or Madam: July 24, 2003 I am interested in your series of books on art history for the young adult. Please send me a catalog of your publications. Sincerely, Edward Murton 268 East Dunphry Road, Oakwood, CO 80110-3215

268 East Dunphry Road

Oakwood, CO 80110-3215

July 24, 2003

Riverside Art Books

314 Donnybrook Drive

St. Louis, MO 63128-2640

Dear Sir or Madam:

I am interested in your series of books on art history for the young adult. Please send me a

catalog of your publications.

Sincerely,

Edward Murton

Index of Skills

Index of Topics
Related to Content Areas